THE I CHONG

MEDITATIONS FROM THE JOINT

BY TOMMY CHONG

SIMON SPOTLIGHT ENTERTAINMENT

NEW YORK   LONDON   TORONTO   SYDNEY

SIMON SPOTLIGHT ENTERTAINMENT

An imprint of Simon & Schuster

1230 Avenue of the Americas, New York, New York 10020

SIMON SPOTLIGHT ENTERTAINMENT and related logo are trademarks of
Simon & Schuster, Inc.

Designed by Steve Kennedy and Greg Stadnyk

Manufactured in the United States of America

First Edition   10   9   8   7   6   5   4   3   2   1

Library of Congress Cataloging-in-Publication Data

Chong, Tommy, 1938–

The I Chong : meditations from the joint / by Tommy Chong.—1st ed.

p.   cm.

ISBN-13: 978-1-4169-1554-6

ISBN-10: 1-4169-1554-0

1. Chong, Tommy, 1938– 2. Prisoners—United States—Biography. 3. Drug
paraphernalia industry—United States. I. Title.

HV9468.C48 2006

365'.6092—dc22

2006008561

*For the millions of victims incarcerated
as a result of the U.S. government's drug laws*

CONTENTS

ONE: Ch'ien / The Creative
Ch'ien / Ch'ien
1

TWO: Shih / The Army
K'un / K'an
26

THREE: Po / Splitting Apart
Kên / K'un
41

FOUR: K'an / The Abysmal (Water)
K'an / K'an
50

FIVE: Ting / The Caldron
Li / Sun
68

SIX: Chên / The Arousing (Shock, Thunder)
Chên / Chên
79

SEVEN: Chieh / Limitation
K'an / Tui
90

EIGHT: Chûn / Difficulty at the Beginning
K'an / Chên
120

NINE: Sung / Conflict
Ch'ien / K'an
126

TEN: Pi / Holding Together (Union)
K'an / K'un
134

ELEVEN: P'i / Standstill (Stagnation)
Ch'ien / K'un
155

TWELVE: Ku / Work On What Has Been Spoiled
Kên / Sun
165

THIRTEEN: Kuan / Contemplation (View)
Sun / K'un
171

FOURTEEN: Fu / Return (The Turning Point)
K'un / Chên
178

FIFTEEN: Ta Ch'u / The Taming Power of the Great
Kên / Ch'ien
182

SIXTEEN: Li / The Clinging, Fire
Li / Li
192

SEVENTEEN: Ch'ien / Modesty
K'un / Kên
198

EIGHTEEN: Shih ho / Biting Through
Li / Chên
204

ACKNOWLEDGMENTS
214

CHAPTER ONE

Ch'ien / The Creative
Ch'ien / Ch'ien

*The Creative is at work; change is in
motion in a dynamic, creative way.*

*This hexagram is also about attaining
the Cosmic viewpoint.*

On May 24, 1938, at approximately 2 a.m. at the
University Hospital Edmonton, Alberta, Canada, I,
Thomas B. Kin Chong, took my very first breath of fresh
Canadian air. I remember thinking, as I yelled in relief,
Now this is some sweet fresh air! It was very stuffy and
crowded in that little womb. My mother, Jean, told me
later that the whole country celebrated my birth with
fireworks and a national holiday—and I totally believed
her because I knew I was special the minute I won the
race against thousands of competing sperm. It was a
very tight race and took a serious lunge at the last

second to win, but I pulled out a victory because I had a strong desire to exist. And believe it or not, I was high on marijuana at the time! As it turns out, my father, the sperm donor, had been smoking a mixture of weed and opium at the time of conception. Luckily, this was before drug testing, so my birth was not contested. In fact, it was celebrated around the world—in England, India, Hong Kong, Australia, New Zealand, Canada, and parts of Africa.

Of course, the fireworks celebration was really for Queen Victoria's birthday. But my mother always wanted us kids to feel special and was known to exaggerate a little bit to achieve her goal. This was understandable given the fact that she was self-taught and could hardly read or write, as she was taken out of school when her mother died suddenly from a self-inflicted wound. However, despite her lack of formal education (she made it to third grade), or perhaps because of it, my mother was a very special lady who had several degrees in the finer arts of life, such as love, compassion, understanding, and generosity.

My father, Stan Chong (original stoner), was born in Canton Alley, which at one time housed the entire Chinese population of Vancouver, Canada, back when anti-Chinese feelings among the white people were at their peak. The street where he was born had to be gated and locked up at night to keep the drunken racists from attacking the Chinese, who were brought in to build the

Canadian Pacific Railway. The Chinese in those days were not even considered human let alone Canadian. They were a cheap labor force and were expected to just disappear when the railroad was finished.

The Canadian government actually had the Chinese workers pay for the cost of the railroad by charging each worker an "entrance fee," which amounted to the total cost of the railroad's construction, in the neighborhood of twenty-five million dollars. And to add insult to injury, the Chinese workers, who single-handedly built every inch of the railroad, were excluded from the official picture at the end. The workers were all fired at the end of the job and given nothing to get them back home to China, leaving others in the Chinese community to form benevolent societies to help feed and clothe the workers.

My mom and dad met and married in Edmonton in 1935, and my brother, Stan Jr., my sister, Nellie, and I soon followed. They were together for more than fifty years, this five-foot-eight gorgeous Irish-Scottish lass and her handsome, athletic, five-foot-three Chinese husband. They met in a city park in Edmonton on a summer's day that year. The park was the place where singles met in those days. The girls would stroll arm in arm past the groups of eligible single Chinese men, giving the eye to the ones who looked promising. Edmonton in the thirties was bustling with immigrants from all countries, with Chinese and Ukrainians being among the most populous. So it wasn't unusual for a beautiful Ukrainian (or Irish-Scottish) girl to hook up with a Chinese guy with absolutely nothing in common in the language department except broken English.

My father, who spoke English with a slight Cantonese accent right up to the time he died, had no problem conversing with my mother. She and my father were the translators between their Ukrainian and Chinese friends, so it was natural that they fell in love and married. She gave birth to my brother the year after they made their vows, with me coming a little more than two years later.

The entire country was in the midst of the Great Depression and work was scarce. Pop was a good hockey player and a pool hustler but a lousy Chinaman because he hung with mostly white and Italian guys. He did what he could to bring home the bacon, but it was tough. He became so desperate, he moved us out to the country where he tried to be a turkey farmer. These were trying times for my mother, as her first home with her cute little Chinese guy was a converted chicken shack replete with the latest in outdoor plumbing. They eventually made it livable, but as he struggled to make a go of the farm, the depression worsened, and we had to move back to Edmonton.

I remember riding on a wagon with our furniture, bedding, and belongings being pulled by a team of horses at night. I also remember our pet crow flying away sometime during the trip. I was still a baby, but when Mom told us how Pop had brought home a baby crow and how she had trained it to be a family pet only to lose it when we made the move back to Edmonton, the memory of that night came to me then as clearly as it does now sixty-seven years later. I can almost smell the horses and the cold, brisk Canadian night as we made our way slowly to the city.

The Second World War was raging and Canada decided to join in, and even though Chinese were not encouraged to join the armed forces, my father, who considered himself a true Canadian, enlisted in the Canadian Artillery and became a gunner on a twenty-five-pound antipersonnel weapon. My mother, along with my brother and me, followed my dad back east to a little town in Nova Scotia, where he completed his basic training.

It was during this time that I experienced my first memory of feeling pain and feeling alive. Up until that moment, I'd been pampered, fed, changed, put to bed, and in general totally shielded from any serious discomfort. But this first experience of pain was intense enough to stay with me to this day.

One night my father brought a couple of his drunken army buddies over to our tiny apartment. Alcohol was considered an important part of war and was encouraged, even supplied to the soldiers, by the central command because it makes the user aggressive and fearless, a combination needed to create an army of cannon fodder. I was asleep in my crib when they came in. I guess my father wanted to show his family off to the soldiers, and one of the drunken idiots thought he'd like to hold a baby, so he reached into the crib and picked me up. The soldier was smoking a cigar at the time and the lit end fell off the cigar and down into my nightgown.

The pain was intense and immediate, so I started screaming at the top of my lungs, which ignited my mother into action. She snatched me up from the drunken fool, tore off my nightshirt, and knocked the still burning ash from my chest. I carried the scar of that night for a good year according to my mother, who could have killed the drunk she was so mad. My memory of the incident, of course, has been magnified by my mother's version, which was embellished each time she told it, but I swear I remember that night as clearly as the trip back to Edmonton. The good thing about this painful memory was that it kept me from ever developing an alcohol problem.

When my dad left for Europe to fight in the war, my mother took her family (including my little sister, whom she was carrying inside her) and went relative-hopping, staying with her many brothers and sisters scattered across Canada. All her kin took her and her little "mixed" kids in, except one older sister: Annabelle. Apparently Annabelle had a problem relating to her brothers and sisters, partly because being one of the oldest girls, she had to be the mother after their mother committed suicide. So when she heard that her little sister had married a Chinese guy and was coming with her half-breed Chinese kids to live with her, she freaked. Annabelle and her husband sold their house and moved out of town just so she wouldn't have to be tainted with our presence.

It seems so trivial now, but in those days mixed marriages were actually illegal in parts of the United States and certainly frowned upon in Canada. I finally met Annabelle years later when she lived close to my mother and father's home on Vancouver Island, off the west coast of British Columbia. She was cordial and polite, but we could see the uncomfortable feeling we still gave her. I was amazed at how much she resembled my mother. They could have been twins, the only difference being her unfounded fear of Chinese.

Mom's half-Chinese children never bothered her poor relatives though, and there were more poor relatives than rich ones like Annabelle, so we always had a place to stay. One of the more exotic places was a trapper's cabin deep in the mountains and forests of British Columbia, where my aunt Lillie (Mom's younger sister) and her husband, Bill, ran a trap line. Uncle Bill, who was Ukrainian, lived and hunted in the wilds like an aborigine, setting traps and collecting and selling the pelts.

It was in this setting that my third vivid memory was created. My uncle Bill was a man of many skills, which enabled him to live deep in the forest without any out-side human contact for months on end. One of his skills was music. He could play the banjo, and although that might not sound like such a big deal now, it was back then. This was a time when it was considered a luxury to have a radio in your house. Hell, it was a luxury to have a house! It's hard to imagine what life would be like without music, especially nowadays, when we have so many music outlets, from radio, CDs, DVDs, and video games to television, live concerts, and on and on. Back then, in the bush . . . nada. The only sounds you heard there were the echoes of your mind, the sounds of silence, and the sounds of the forests and rivers—the sounds of Mother Nature. So when Uncle Bill played his banjo, it was party time.

One night when I was about two years old, Bill had just put his banjo away and was heading into the bush to check his trap lines. I followed him because I wanted more of that banjo sound. When Uncle Bill took off on his dogsled, nobody noticed me toddling after him, trip-ping along in my flannel pj's, I guess because I was so tiny.

When Mom realized I was missing, she freaked, as did everyone else, because we were in wild animal coun-try. They ransacked the cabin looking for me, thinking I had crawled into some nook or cranny. Meanwhile, I was hiking down the trail as fast as my little legs would carry me. I soon tired and found a flat stump to rest awhile, and that's where they eventually found me. I was curled up, fast asleep, with the pet dog that had stayed with me the whole time.

I remember being woken up with a lot of yelling and being carried back to the cabin. I loved being carried; it was such a comforting feeling. My mom would tell this story to us when we were growing up, and as with most of her stories, each time she told it, the event got bigger.

But the memory that perhaps sticks out the most was the day my father came home from the war. We were living with mom's oldest sister, Aunt Jessie, and her family in Trail, BC. I remember playing with a lacrosse ball, bouncing it against the cement wall near the house, when he appeared. He was dressed in his Canadian Army uniform and carrying his duffel bag. My twin cousins were holding my dad's hands, and I remember them telling him, "There he is."

The last time my father had seen me was in Nova Scotia, when his army buddy burned me with the cigar. That was almost four years before. He smelled like the cologne they give men at the barbershop as he picked me up, only to put me down because I was a "big boy." It felt uncomfortable being treated like a baby. Hell, I was big. I could bounce a lacrosse ball against the wall and catch it.

When Pop returned, he moved us to Calgary, where the army had a hospital for veterans of the war. Pop had some problems with his teeth and some other war-related injuries. Mom had health problems of her own, serious health problems. She had contracted TB from her sister Lillie, who lived in the bush and had been infected by the local Indians, who had been infected by the white people. Ironic, when you think of it.

We all lived in a tiny room over a Chinese restaurant on Central Avenue in Chinatown with the distinct smell of Chinese food—the soy sauce and garlic and black beans—wafting up from the kitchen below. I used to crawl out on the tar roof in front of our room to watch people walk on the crowded street below. There was a vacant lot next door where my brother and I played. We found Coke bottles that were worth two cents if we turned them in.

Mom had to be taken to the TB hospital and put in the isolation ward, where the doctors practiced Canadian medicine on her. They had to remove her left lung to stop the disease. Medicine that would have made the procedure unnecessary was available in the States, but apparently not in Canada.

Pop was having his health problems too, so he had to find somewhere to put us kids. There were three of us now; my little sister, Nellie, was born while Pop was overseas. I had contracted pleurisy, another lung disease. Lucky for me, they were able to treat my condition with penicillin and other antibiotic drugs. I could have been treated at home, but we didn't have a home, so I was put in the Children's General Hospital, where I remained for six months. It was an enjoyable stay with clean sheets every day and beautiful nurses who spoiled the hell out of me because I was a "cute little brown guy."

This was when I found out it was cool to be brown and cute. All the nurses would take turns hugging me. And believe me, as small as I was, I still appreciated soft breasts being squeezed against my little body. One red-headed nurse would make a point of getting her hug every morning just before she gave me two needles in the butt. Two needles, and man, it hurt, because they had to inject the stuff slowly into the muscle. The pain was masked with the nice smelling soft breasts of the redheaded nurse. (I guess that's what made me a sucker for titties!) As the needles went in I can remember looking out the window at the kids playing baseball in the park below while us sick kids were cooped up in a hospital room wishing we were out there with them.

Once I made a full recovery, I was taken from the hospital and put into a "home," the Salvation Army Booth Memorial Home. It was an orphanage that took in abused, illegitimate, and abandoned children, and although we were none of those things, we needed a place to live because my mother was still in the sanatorium and my father was in the veteran's hospital recovering from his World War II wounds. The home held about a hundred or so kids, from infants to sixteen-year-olds, and it was run like a prison.

This was my first prison experience. And the memories of my home stay are etched deeply in my mind from my first day right up to the last. My father, who was on leave from the hospital, took me into a sunlit office and I was then led out into a tiny garden while he enrolled me. I was given a coloring book and crayons, which I immediately went to work on. I loved coloring and was pretty good at it. I learned in the hospital, where we colored for hours. I stayed within the lines, and I used all the good colors.

After about thirty minutes, I was led back into the office, where I was told to say good-bye to my father. I didn't cry because I was used to being left at places, like the hospital and relative's homes. This was normal for me. My father handed me a bag of new clothes that he had purchased and a stack of my favorite comic books and told me to be a good boy. As he left, a lady smiled and shook his hand, assuring him that they'd "take good care of little Tommy."

But as soon as he was gone, the lady's demeanor changed abruptly. She took my bag of clothes and my comics and put them on her desk. She then walked out of the room, ordering me to follow her. We walked up some stairs and into a room with rows of cots, which were divided by wooden clothes closets. I was assigned a bed and given "home clothes" to wear. The clothes were patched up jeans and frayed ragged shirts and some baggy fitting underwear. I stripped out of my nice clothes and put on the rags. I never saw my new clothes or my comics again.

That night I met my fellow campers. They were a rowdy, raggedy, wild bunch of kids with whom I immediately identified. They were playing a game of climbing onto the dressers and jumping onto their beds. I was invited to try. I watched the others for a while and then got up enough nerve to try, but as soon as I climbed onto the dresser, the mean lady came busting in the door. All the other boys knew that she'd be coming, but I was caught high and dry.

The lady pulled me from my perch and yanked me down the stairs to her office. She told me to hold out my hand. I wasn't prepared for the leather strap that she smacked my hands with, and the pain shot through my body like electricity. I was so surprised I didn't cry. I don't think I even cried out. I was stunned. This was the first time I had been hit by an adult. She smacked me again and my hands felt like they were on fire. Then she yanked me around and put her face right next to mine and quietly whispered, "Now you go to bed and quit fooling around, or you'll get twice as much next time!"

I started up the stairs and stumbled halfway up. My hands stopped my fall, but the grit on the stairs increased the throbbing pain in my hands and the tears came. I crawled into bed and silently cried myself to sleep. The next morning I was introduced to the eating arrangements at the home. Sunday was the day we were served buttered toast. However, if you did not grab your share right away, you missed out. The older and bigger kids ran the show, taking toys and food from the weaker ones while the staff ignored their abuses.

We also had to endure long hours of religious indoctrination. Saying grace went on forever until whatever appetite you might have come in with was gone. I was used to being served in bed on trays in the hospital and now I was at the mercy of the older kids. Luckily, my brother was one of the older kids and he watched out for me the whole time we were there.

The food was disgusting—I found maggots in the oatmeal a few times; peas felt like marbles, hard and uneatable—but it was the constant praying before the meals that really turned me off. Singing was mandatory and one song in particular stood out to me—"Onward, Christian Soldiers." The lyrics are so anti-Jesus that when you think of how warlike that song is, you have to wonder just what Christ they are referring to. The song begins, "Onward, Christian soldiers, marching as to war, with the cross of Jesus going on before." These lyrics put the Prince of Peace at the head of an army marching off to forcibly convert people. This was not the Jesus I would come to learn about later, but the Salvation Army Booth Memorial Home was the only orphanage in Calgary at the time, so we had to endure these attempts at religious brainwashing.

My brother had to attend the nearby public school,

where he endured even more humiliation on a daily basis. Every lunch hour the home kids were told to stand beside their desks to receive their daily milk ration. This distribution could have been done in a more discreet manner; it was as if the school wanted to humiliate and degrade the home kids. Of course, there were fistfights with the so-called normal kids, and my brother had to become one of the toughest kids in Calgary because of his stay at the home. Fistfights in those days were very brutal, especially when there was no one around to break them up. I guess the cold weather fueled the fighting vibe.

My father eventually bought a little cottage on the edge of town with some help from the army. It was a two-bedroom cottage with an outdoor toilet that the locals called an outhouse. Pop built a new and improved outhouse, enlisted the help of mom's sister Lillie, sprung his kids from the orphanage, and took us home. Our little house seemed like a palace to me, and even though it had outdoor plumbing and was heated by a wood-burning kitchen stove, it was our home.

Mom was still stuck in the TB sanatorium, where we still were not allowed to visit her. However, she would have Pop bring us to the building so she could see us from the window of her hospital room. It would be another year before we had a mom to hug, but we were a family again and we had a home.

We lived in our little hippie home for seven years and

attended a little, one-room red schoolhouse. The school was so crowded that we had to split the days among the students, with us young ones attending in the morning and the older ones in the afternoon. One of my most vivid memories of school was reading headlines that showed Japan being hit with atomic bombs to end World War II. I was seven years old that historic day and I remember thinking, *Wow, that's a big bomb!*

My dad loved going to movies, especially drive-ins, because we brought our own food and he didn't have to pay for popcorn. And my favorite part of that experience was the newsreel footage of the war. The horror and destruction seemed so normal to my young mind; guns and violence had become part of the make-believe world of our childhood.

The serial Westerns starred actors like Roy Rogers and Gene Autry, the role models of the day. I laugh when I think back on how each episode would have some pithy message about "being good boys and girls"—this, after an hour of killing Indians and bad outlaws. I remember playing Cowboys and Indians and always wanting to be Roy Rogers, although both my brother and I looked more Indian, with our suntans and mixed features.

I might have been a "cowboy" in our make-believe world, but I was pure Indian in real life. I learned how to throw knives and hatchets. I made my own bow and arrows, and hunted field mice. We would often hike into the foothills that lay to the west of our little cottage, carrying a lunch and matches to make a campfire. Once we found a nice grove of trees, we would gather rocks for the campfire and gather dead wood for the fuel. Then we'd spend most of the day climbing the trees.

Sometimes a friend would join us and a few times I went by myself. The beauty of the summer day was so overwhelming that I would have to lie down in the middle of a field and listen to the singing of the insects and the birds. The smell of the grass and occasional flowers would intoxicate me, and I would feel one with the Earth, suspended in time. The walk home was always memorable because of our incredible thirst. We almost always neglected to bring enough water or we used it all to put out the campfire. In any case, we would be dying of thirst as we crossed the large flat cow pasture, which made it feel like we were crossing a desert with the hot summer sun beating down.

Our destination was the well pump at the edge of the cow pasture, where fresh ice-cold water from the ground would quench our thirst and cool our heads. The taste of that water stays with me to this day, so fresh and clear with not a trace of chemicals, and so life-giving to the desert wanderers. I also remember the words to "Cool Water" by Sons of the Pioneers running through my mind on repeat every time I hit the pump: "All day I face the barren waste without the taste of water . . . cool water."

My life during that time was filled with the wonder and joys of youth. Although we never had an abundance of money or property, we had the love of a strong-willed mother and father and the entire countryside to roam carefree. The weather in Calgary was as extreme as the Arctic, with really long, hot summer days followed by a crisp fall into a long, cold winter. Those months in a cottage heated by a small kitchen woodstove gave us all a sense of pride in knowing we could survive a Calgary winter.

The second year in our little house my brother and I trekked across open fields and pasture to the school, which was located a good mile and a half from our house. The ranch kids rode horses to school—an idea that might sound romantic these days, but then we felt sorry for those kids because of all the extra work they had to do for their horses. They had to brush them down, feed and water them, and lead them into the stables all before school.

The neighborhood bully rode a horse to school and once in a while he would offer us a ride. I accepted once and as soon as I got on the horse he kicked it in the flanks and the horse bucked me off. He got a big laugh at us morons who fell for his stupid jokes every time— everyone except my brother, that is.

The first time we met the bully was at the corner store that was owned and operated by his mother. We were the new kids in the neighborhood, so he immediately picked a fight with me. I had no idea how to fight so I ended up on the bottom with the bully smacking me in my face. Suddenly I felt the bully fly off of me, then I glimpsed a flash of my brother jumping on the guy and smacking the shit out of him. The kid immediately became our best friend after that, and other than getting bucked from his horse now and then, we were cool.

Stan clearly took after my father, who was the toughest guy of his size I had ever met. He was short but he had the heart of a tiger. When his mother split from my grandfather, she moved the family from Vancouver to Edmonton. On his first day of school Pop had a run-in with the class bully, who tried to push him around. Pop dropped him like a bad habit with one punch and then jammed the bully's head under the steel frame that bolted the seat to the floor. They had to call the janitor to remove the seat and free the guy, and then take him to the hospital to have his ear sewn back onto his head.

The fact that we were "mixed kids from the home" invited rude comments from various bigoted idiots who populated Calgary at the time. And, of course, the comments would provoke a violent response from my brother, who developed quite a fearful reputation in Calgary. He played semiretarded pro hockey in an industrial league with nutcases who were banned from playing in the professional leagues because they were too violent. The games were played outdoors and the refs did not break up fights. They would fight till someone got hurt badly or they both got too tired to fight. I could handle myself with my friends, but having an older brother who could beat the shit out of me whenever he felt like it kept me real. The lesson: No matter how tough you are, there is someone who can whip your ass.

But thankfully, I was steered into the right path when I was invited to a summer camp for poor, raggedy-ass kids run by a church group. Bible camp changed my life forever. My brother and I were returning home from a friend's house when a large Chevrolet sedan came up the road and stopped alongside us. The lady and the man in the car asked if we were from the area, to which we replied, "Yeah, why?"

My brother kept walking, but I was intrigued when the couple explained that they ran a camp where they teach you about the Bible. They told us that the camp was located on a lake where kids could swim and fish, and they had bonfires at night where they'd sit around and sing. I did not hesitate a beat; I told them to sign me up! My brother was ready to go as well, most likely swayed by the prospect of having new people to beat up.

The bible camp people drove us home to get our mom's written permission and, just like that, we were on our way to camp. I was in heaven for the next ten days. We were divided by age into various groups with each group assigned a teacher. The teacher would take us into the woods to a meadow where we would sit and be taught Bible stories. The stories were about love, understanding, forgiveness, and how Jesus healed the sick and gave sight to the blind. The stories were riveting, and the setting made them even more relevant because of the beauty of nature. The teachers taught only the gentle, sweet, healing stories from the Bible, leaving the brutal parts for the adults.

But it was the nighttime prayer that really changed my life during those ten days at camp. We all had to say a prayer individually before we went to sleep and it had to come from the heart. When it was my turn, I said a prayer that came from deep within my soul. It was as if someone else was talking for me, saying things that I had not even thought about. The spontaneity and that feeling from above in my prayer took me to a feeling that surpasses understanding. I guess it was a feeling of connection to the Higher Power. I was filled with that feeling throughout the week, and when it was time to go home, I was given another surprise.

During our last meal together, the camp leader was announcing the various awards won by the different groups. I was standing, trying to reach across the table for the food like a little hillbilly kid, when he announced my name as the "best-liked boy."

"Keep standing, Tommy," were the words he used. I didn't hear him at first, but all the kids started clapping when he called my name. I was embarrassed and completely taken off guard. Had I known I was going to receive an award I would have worn a shirt. The nicest boy award. Who gives out an award like that? I should have brought it to the attention of the judge who sentenced me to nine months in jail.

My life has changed considerably since Bible camp, but my knowledge of the power of prayer has been my guiding light since that time. Knowing how to pray has saved my butt countless times. The secret of prayer is expressing gratitude for our existence. And the Truth is, everything happens for a reason. We exist on this plane for a reason. We are here to learn, and we only learn from our mistakes. *Every now and then I have no conscious control over what is written. Most of the spiritual content comes to me, uncontrollable and unexplainable.*

When you give thanks for your blessings with an open heart, great things will happen for you and those you love. Now remember, everyone is on their own separate path (learning from mistakes), and we must always respect that. So when you pray, ask for wisdom and understanding. Don't bother asking for anything else, because if you have wisdom and understanding you don't need anything else.

Now, that is a profound statement that needs to be repeated: If you have wisdom and understanding, you don't need anything else. Life is like playing chess. You cannot play the game unless you know the rules. If you understand the rules you will be able to play, and because it's a game, you know that you will win some and you will lose some, depending on your own wisdom and understanding. This applies to our lives as well.

Notice I said "our lives"? This world we live in is our world. We share with our neighbors. And neighbors are not just fellow human beings; they include every thing in this universe—the air we breathe, the water we drink, and the earth that provides our food. We are never alone because God (life) is with us always, until the end of eternity. God is our very essence, our breath, our blood, our bodies, and our minds; we are "of God." And it is our understanding of this Truth that sets us free.

Now, the question is, free to do what? Free to steal from our neighbors? Free to lie to our neighbors? Free to cheat our neighbors? Free to bully our neighbors? Free to imprison our neighbors? Free to invade our neighbors? Free to commit violent acts against our neighbors? Free to digress from this book and go on a religious rant? Yes! Yes we are free to make mistakes! Because we only learn from our mistakes. We live in a physical world where everything has an opposite, and the opposite of Truth is error. There can be countless errors but only one Truth. So we must remember that through the knowledge of the existence of God, we are free from the ignorance that creates all negative feelings. And the opposite of God is nothing—because God is everything!

When we know for a fact that God exists then we

know that all the negative, evil, horrible thoughts are mistaken illusions created by our own false sense of self (ego) and, in reality, do not exist. These illusions are to be ignored and not given life through accepting them. The Truth is, errors like fear, violence, and murder are committed through ignorance. This is why the only proper prayer is one of gratitude for your knowledge to ask for wisdom and understanding. And like the Bible states, "Ask and ye shall receive."

The I Ching (the Chinese Book of Changes) says, "Great power is best displayed when not used." This is perhaps the greatest example of understanding that I have been given. My own private prayer is one of thanks for my life. My life has been one exciting adventure after another. The land of milk and honey that Moses wandered around the desert looking for exists only in the mortal mind. It is the mortal mind that creates limits to what it thinks we should do, the ego-created mind that fears the shadows yet does not want to turn on a light. We have to learn to embrace experiences and learn from them, both the good ones and the so-called bad ones.

We are here to experience life and to learn to be thankful for our experiences regardless of how brutal they might be. Pain is a reminder that we are alive. Apparently there is no pain when you are dead, so enjoy the pain now, for pain will help lead us to understanding and growth. I have been blessed with the knowledge of my existence. It has been a search that only becomes more and more exciting, and leads me to give thanks without ceasing.

The events described in the following pages were answers to my prayers, as I asked for wisdom and understanding. I wanted to fully understand why I am here and what I am supposed to be doing. The answer came to me in an unexpected but understandable manner.

CHAPTER TWO

Shih / The Army
K'un / K'an

Prepare for a "war"—
a test about to take place.

The morning of February 24, 2003, at 5:30 a.m. in my home in the Pacific Palisades, California, an event happened that changed my life forever. I was asleep at the time, having a wonderfully weird dream—the kind that makes you want to sleep long enough to find out how it ends. I dreamt that I was with beautiful naked women, who were all trying to attack me sexually, and more naked women were outside banging on the glass door demanding to be let in. My wife nudged me awake with her foot and whispered softly, "There's someone banging at the door."

Unsure if I was awake and responding to my wife's words or still dreaming and answering the call of the naked ladies, I got out of bed and made my way down the stairs. I crossed over to the glass front door where I could see a group of armed men wearing helmets and visors standing on the landing. They looked like a group of oversize trick-or-treaters in alien costumes.

One of the men yelled at me to open the door. For a brief moment, I thought, *They must be going from door to door warning people of some impending disaster, or maybe an Enron executive has escaped and is running wild,* so I opened the door. And as I did the armed men rushed into my house and started going from room to room shouting orders at each other.

The leader handed me a piece of paper and informed me, "This is a raid. And this is a search warrant giving us the right to seize what is listed on the warrant."

I took the paper and tried to read it, but without my reading glasses it was just a blur. In fact, the whole raid was a blur!

One of the men yelled at me, "Is there anyone else in the house?"

I answered, "My wife is upstairs." By this time my wife had slipped on a robe and was coming down the stairs, asking me what was going on.

"I think we are being raided."

"What for?" She replied halfway down the stairs.

"I don't know. They won't tell me," I answered back.

"We will tell you in a minute," the leader replied.

Shelby joined me at the bottom of the stairs, and we

watched the armed men run from room to room yelling "clear."

"This is just like a movie," Shelby said. I looked at her and saw excitement in her face. My wife always amazes me with the absolute cool with which she handles everything. She even gave birth to our three children in a very cool way. She is always under control in panic situations. Little things like losing her favorite sweater will send her to therapy immediately, but a situation like having her house raided by twenty or so armed men was really no big deal.

"This is not a movie! This is the real thing!" the leader shouted. He seemed to be sticking close to us to see how we were reacting.

"So, are we under arrest?" my fearless wife shot back.

"No, you are not under arrest," the leader replied.

"So what's going on?" asked Shelby, not the least bit afraid.

I was standing there shivering in my shorts, but I tried to regain my composure and act like the man of the house. "Uh, yeah! What is going on?" I asked.

"We'll tell you soon enough," the leader replied. He hovered around us, directing his men as they searched the house. Shelby went back upstairs to get dressed, while I stood and shivered next to the leader.

"Do you have any drugs?" he asked.

I looked at him for a beat, thinking, *This can't be about drugs, can it?*

"Yeah, I have some pot," I answered, still shaking like a wet puppy, while thinking, *Of course I have pot in the house. I'm Tommy Chong!*

"If you tell us where the drugs are it will go faster."

"Let me think." *Well, I know I have a big bud in the basement and some homegrown up in my office and a taste in the kitchen, now where else?* The cop looked at me with a big smirk on his face. I could see I was making his day.

"I better call a lawyer," I said, not knowing what else to say.

"You don't need a lawyer," he answered back.

I don't need a lawyer? I thought to myself. I was a bit amazed by his response, because in every movie I've ever seen, the perp always refuses to talk to the cops until he sees his lawyer.

"You are not under arrest," he answered back, still smirking. "We will tell you when you can call your lawyer."

I felt weird. *Something is not right here,* I thought. *I'm not under arrest, yet armed men and women in uniform are ransacking my home like World War II Nazi storm troopers.* Dressed in military gear with automatic weapons strapped to their sides, they were running from room to room, carrying armfuls of computers to a vehicle outside, while helicopters hovered in the sky over our house. Was I dreaming? Or had I somehow been transported to Iraq, where this identical scene was being played out repeatedly as America attacked the tiny Arab country with full military force?

"Take Mr. Chong upstairs and have him put on some clothes," the leader ordered one of his men. I guess he was tired of looking at my morning hard-on. I was escorted upstairs and walked into the closet, where my clothes from the previous night awaited me. As I reached for my blue jeans, the armed guard took the clothes from my hands and expertly searched the pockets. He found my pocket knife and laid it on the dresser.

"Sorry, I'm just doing my job," he muttered, almost to himself.

I noticed that many of the armed raiders were embarrassed and would not make eye contact with me. They seemed puzzled and embarrassed as the raid progressed. They all knew me as one half of the comedy team Cheech and Chong, America's favorite stoner comedians. We had entertained them with our records and movies dating back to 1971. Some if not all of the raiders had grown up with our crazy stoner comedy that made what they were doing totally ridiculous.

As I slipped on my pants and shirt the guard casually asked if I had any weapons. Of course, I told him the truth: "No, I do not have any weapons! I don't believe in violence."

My answer did not seem to satisfy him, so he continued to rummage around the closet until he found our small cash box. He asked me for the key. I dug it out of our secret hiding place and handed it to him. He then ushered me downstairs where he reported to the leader.

"I found it," he said quietly. The leader and the guard made eye contact. They were quite pleased with themselves until they opened it and found cash and jewelry but no weapons. Thinking back, I now realize how badly they wanted to find a weapon, any weapon! They were happy to find the cash, but it was the weapon that could have gotten me a substantial jail sentence. I could have and probably would have received ten years in jail had I been in possession of a gun that day, even if it was properly registered.

Thank God I don't believe in guns. They scare the shit out of me. I believe that guns have a vibe of their own and will attack you when you least expect it. The three years I spent in the Canadian Army Cadets taught me all I needed to know about weapons of human destruction. I've seen what guns can do to people, especially when they think they are not loaded. And it's always the stupid people (Dick Cheney) who get hurt or hurt someone else by not respecting guns. Like one idiot in the army cadets who held a match to a live round to see what would happen. He lost his thumb and finger finding out. Now *that* was stupid.

The beautiful thing about comedy is that no matter what happens we comics always see the funny side. In the middle of the raid I had to take a shit, but when I started for the toilet, the guard told me to halt. I let him in on my predicament and he told me I'd have to wait until his boss gave me the okay. Luckily for all concerned, the boss told him to let me do my business but to go with me. I told him I didn't think that would be such a good idea. I'm sixty-six years old, and being anywhere near an old man when he takes a morning shit could ruin a man forever. They took my word for it and I was allowed a private dump.

As I stood in my own foyer surrounded by all these gun-toting agents, my initial shock subsided and I was no longer the least bit frightened. I knew we had done nothing illegal. Our glass factory in Gardena, California, was a legal operation. We were an incorporated company paying our fair share of state and federal taxes. In fact, the company was undergoing an audit the day of the raid.

So what was the problem? Weed? Oh, that. Yes, they did find almost a pound of grass that morning. It took them a couple of hours, but they found the weed that was given to me by my fans and for which I had a legal prescription from my doctor. The prescription was for my own personal medical problem, which was . . . stress brought on by shit like this!

Ironically, weed was never listed on the Feds' search warrant. The DEA raid captain had to hand write an addendum to the warrant that he had me sign. The whole operation was strange indeed. So the question of the day that had yet to be answered: What horrendous crime had I committed that took all these guys with the helicopters and the flack jackets and the automatic weapons and God knows what else to terrorize my wife and me? The leader, sensing the time was right, announced the reason for the raid.

"Bongs," he said.

"Bongs?" I repeated.

The DEA leader looked at me, his smirk getting bigger. He cleared his throat and announced in a rehearsed manner, much like a wimpy news anchorman, "Chong Glass and Nice Dreams Enterprises are the targets of this expensive and dangerous early morning raid, which was part of a nationwide raid on bong companies across America, called Operation Pipe Dreams."

This "crime-stopping" event that was being filmed by all the major television networks was the "brainchild" of the attorney general of the United States, who was announcing the details as the raids were being conducted.

"Bongs?" I repeated. I really must have been dreaming. "You mean all this is about bongs?"

The leader had a look on his face that really pissed me off. He had that shit-eating grin that you see in movies when the bad guy announces to the world that it was he all along.

"You motherfucker!" I spit out the words automatically. The armed narcs moved in on me, expecting violence. "You motherfucker," I said quietly to the leader, who now sported a huge grin on his white hillbilly face.

One of his men started moving objects from the glass coffee table, anticipating a brawl or some sort of altercation. I noticed the guy was Chinese and that the raiding party was mixed racially and otherwise. Black, white, Asian, female, gay. It was a politically correct raiding party. Of course! It was beginning to make sense! This was really a "political raid." The U.S. government was in fact continuing its policy of "war" on its own people. The thinly disguised War on Drugs is, in fact, a war on the hippie culture and on the poor, black, and brown people of America.

The events of 9/11 suddenly gave the "devil worshipping" Christian Right a reason to attack and imprison anyone and everyone who did not subscribe to their narrow racist neo-Nazi Christian beliefs. The Chinese guy dressed in the DEA raiding outfit was the poster boy for the repressive Republican society that now ruled America. All those dire warnings about Big Brother that we were given repeatedly during the sixties, seventies, and eighties had become reality. The question in my mind now is, did we create these events by worrying about them, or did we predict them and that made them happen?

"You can call your lawyer now," the leader said, breaking the tension in the room.

My wife and I looked at each other. Who should we call? My mind was blank. I couldn't think of a single person to call. Ironically, almost all our neighbors in the

Palisades are lawyers, and Shelby's friend's husband is probably the best entertainment lawyer in Hollywood, yet we couldn't think of anyone to call.

"I guess we better call Joe Mannis," I said finally.

Joe was a divorce lawyer, who also represented me with the movie studios when Cheech and I did the movies during the early eighties. We got Joe on the telephone, and the DEA leader talked to him for about ten minutes before handing me the phone.

"How are you doing?" was Joe's first question. Without waiting for a reply, he continued, "Okay, here is what is happening. They are raiding you because of Chong Glass. They're going to offer you a deal. And they are not going to arrest you, although they could. Actually, they can do anything they want—they're the federal government." Joe continued talking, but his words just faded into the background as I began to realize the extent and scope of the situation.

I handed the telephone to my wife and started talking to the leader of the pack, who was suddenly acting very chummy. Soon we were chatting away like old friends. I fell for it hook, line, and sinker. But since I believed that I had done nothing wrong, I didn't feel the need to censor myself . . . even with the guy in riot gear who'd just finished ransacking my house. Man, was I stupid!

I talked and talked, telling him (and anyone else within ear shot) how the weed laws were unconstitutional and how hemp will save the world some day. I spouted the same hippie logic that I had been espousing for almost forty years. "Blah, blah, blah, should be legal, blah, blah, it helps people with AIDS and MS, blah, blah, it's way safer than alcohol or tobacco, blah, blah."

Looking back now I see how incredibly out of touch I was. There I was doing my stoner act for a guy who seemed to think every doper, hippie bastard was the son of the devil and should be rounded up and exterminated as soon as possible. I was Anne Frank talking to Herr Mengele. He let me go on and on, looking at me with that concerned *I know what you mean* look on his face, while I dug my grave deeper and deeper.

Eventually, Shelby got fed up and announced that she was ready for her morning coffee. One of the cops actually told her, "Well, there's the kitchen. Go make some." I winced when I heard him talk to her that way—not just because of the sexist overtones, but because Shelby has a very low tolerance for this kind of bullshit, especially coming from a cop who was in the middle of raiding her home. *Here we go,* I thought.

But to my surprise, her response was mild. "Excuse me, there is a princess on board here. I need my Starbucks," she replied lightheartedly.

"Well, you will have to wait until we are finished here," the cop responded.

"Does that mean we are under arrest?" she countered.

"No, you are not under arrest. You can leave, but

you can't come back until we are finished," he said, getting a little pissed at being challenged.

"Well, then, can you move your cars? I don't want you to scare off my housekeeper," replied the princess.

The cop looked to his boss for direction. The leader sensed he was losing control over the situation and was about to say something when one of the cops appeared from the basement with a box of bamboo pipes. They were part of the collection of pipes that I had on display at an art show a few months earlier. I mentioned the highly publicized show to the leader, who informed me that he had attended it and was amazed at some of the prices the art was fetching.

"You were at the show?" I asked, flattered.

"We have been following you around for a year now," he replied.

"You guys were at the head shop in Arlington, Texas," I almost shouted. "I remember talking to you."

The leader smiled almost sheepishly. I remembered them because they looked like big, clumsy, undercover DEA agents. And one of the girls who worked at the store had followed them around wearing a DEA T-shirt! Of course, none of the folks who worked at the head shop thought anything of the five jocks wearing backpacks carrying hidden cameras and microphones.

I had stopped by to sign Chong bongs for the customers. The leader, posing as a fan, and I went outside for a little private chat. He asked me if my bongs were really used for smoking pot and why my bongs or any bongs were superior to other pipes. Of course, I was honest and told him everything. I wasn't worried about speaking so freely because I hadn't been mirandized, nor had I done anything wrong. Pro that I am, I spoke directly into the hidden camera/recorder in his backpack. You see what smoking pot will do to you?

The DEA finally wrapped up the raid at our house at around ten a.m. They had been playing cops and plunderers for almost five hours now and everyone was tired. Joe Mannis arrived and informed me he had contacted Richard Hirsch, a famous criminal lawyer, who I knew from World Gym. I felt good knowing that I had a top lawyer and a friend working on my behalf. *Hey, they can't do this to me,* I thought. *I'll smoke them in court. As popular as I am, people will pay money to be on the jury. Chong on trial for selling bongs? This will be a slam dunk. No jury in America would dare convict me, not for bongs. . . . Yeah, right!*

We contacted our son Paris, who was aware of the raid because the federal agents were busy raiding the factory at the same time our house was being raided. They woke up Brian, the factory manager, and had him drive out to the factory to open the doors. Once inside, the agents confiscated some of the finished glass pipes and smashed the unfinished ones. They carted away all the computers and some office files, while trashing the rest of the place for no apparent reason. For the first time, I felt like I could really understand what the European Jews suffered under Hitler, and this was all happening in America in 2003.

The Bush people were on a mission, a crusade, ever since the events of 9/11. The terrorist acts suddenly gave the Bush administration carte blanche to act in any manner they wanted. The Republicans seized on the opportunity to forward their own agenda. The people of the United States lost more than the World Trade Center and countless loved ones that fateful day. We lost our freedom. That act of terrorism gave too much power to a group of right-wing Christian devil worshippers ready to demonize and destroy anyone standing in their way.

Now, lest you think I'm being hyperbolic, hear me out. I call these people devil worshippers for this reason: Their own Christian Bible states, "It shall be according to thy faith," meaning, if you believe in something— even if it is not real—it will become real to you because of your belief. So if you believe that the devil exists, this illusion that you create will stay with you until it is erased by the rebirth of your perception of the Truth! And the Truth is, God is real and everything made by God is good. Evil and the so-called devil are illusions created by organized religion to give them an enemy to protect their "sheep" from.

I find it interesting that hell is associated with eternal fire. How can that be bad? My version of hell would be darkness and cold. I like warmth! Like the Indian sweat lodge: Water is poured over hot stones to heat the hut with steam, and this is the Native American version of heaven. It is a place to commune with the Father—an experience as spiritual, fulfilling, and as far from hell as one could get.

Hell, to me, is sitting in an uncomfortable pew being bored silly by some religious fanatic trying to justify his pedophilic activities in the name of Jesus Christ.

On that morning of the raid, I was made the enemy of the Republican Christian Right. In the interest of protecting their sheep, the government selected me—Tommy Chong, dangerous stoner, comedian—as the poster boy for their Big Brother campaign. It would be laughable if it weren't true. . . .

CHAPTER THREE

Po / Splitting Apart
Kên / K'un

*Disbelief in the power of nonaction,
or in the power of "just being."*

The press had been invited along by the DEA, so the news hit America and the world as the raids were going on. Although more than fifty bong sites were raided that morning, it seemed that mine was the only one featured in the news reports. The news spread rapidly throughout the world, and I began hearing from people I had not heard from in years—people like Rickey Morris from Calgary, a guy I ran with during my wild teenage years. Rickey called up as soon as he heard his old friend was in trouble.

"You okay?" he asked when I answered the phone. I had to smile because he had the same concern in his voice that he had back in the fifties, when we used to go to dances and after-hour parties, where we would brawl if we were not allowed in.

"Yeah, I'm fine. . . . It's gonna be okay," I replied.

"Okay, call me if you need anything."

My brother, Stan, called from Vancouver Island, where he lived and worked as a security guard. "Hey, brother, you okay? We saw you on TV. . . . What's going on?"

"Oh, nothing much," I replied. "Just a little problem with the Feds. . . . No big deal! How you doing?" My big brother had suffered a couple of heart attacks in the past few years and had to drastically change his lifestyle.

"Oh, I'm okay!" he replied. "I can't complain. So what's gonna happen to you?"

I remembered then how my big brother would always beat up anyone who messed with me, and I envisioned him slapping the shit out of John Ashcroft. It was a comforting image.

I also got a call from a Canadian jazz musician whom I had not heard from in years; in fact, I was seventeen years old the last time I saw him. I remember that moment because he did something that changed my life forever. He had been down in Los Angeles checking out the jazz clubs, and when I saw him afterward, he had presents for me. He handed me a Lenny Bruce record and a huge marijuana joint! It was by far the nicest present I had ever received from anyone.

I went home and, after smoking a tiny bit of the joint, put on the record and proceeded to laugh harder than I had ever laughed before. I was participating in a ritual that millions of kids would later repeat—only with a

Cheech and Chong record instead of the Lenny Bruce. The joint lasted me for almost a month, maybe longer, and I still have the Lenny Bruce record. What a turn-on! I only hope that someday I can repay him for the beautiful gifts.

Quite a few of my shady gangster friends got in touch with me, but, surprisingly, none of my straight lawyer friends called. Cheech's manager, David Goldman, however, did call . . . to let me know that the movie deal we had with Revolution had fallen through. Oh yeah, all the bad-news bearers called, telling me that other projects—some voice-over work—had been canceled. I even got a call from the Feds. At least, I assume it was the Feds checking up on me. Some lady called pretending to be a news reporter and asked if I thought I was being treated fairly by the government. I assumed it was a setup because she knew details that only a Fed would know. So I was polite, but I hung up as soon as I could. It occurred to me then that my phone may have been tapped for months! But I was ready to fight back. I was not going down without a fight!

We met at Richard Hirsch's office in Santa Monica early the next day. Brian, Paris, Shelby, and I were ushered into Mike Nasatir's office, where we waited for Richard and Joe. Richard poked his head in and asked to see me alone for a moment. We exchanged pleasantries and then Richard went into concerned lawyer mode, asking if Brian was part of the glass company ownership. When I said he was just an employee, Richard indicated that it would be preferable that he not be present.

Once Brian was dismissed, the meeting began with Richard telling us that he and Mike had met with the California head of narcotics, who told them that he himself had not known of the law we were accused of breaking, but that the law did exist and the government had launched a nationwide operation to shut down the bong industry. And because I was the most visible and most famous, I was to be given an offer I couldn't refuse.

The federal statute that I violated had been on the books since 1994 but was ignored by the Feds in virtually every state because of the difficulty of enforcing it. The law states that it is a violation if one makes or ships drug paraphernalia across state lines. Our glass company was unique because we made art that sold at gallery shows. But the Feds had the law on the books especially for people like myself who want to educate people on the medical value of this fantastic herb. So I felt I had a good chance of having my side of the weed debate heard. The law that I "broke" enables right-wing demi-slobs to act in any fashion they choose when it comes to people who oppose them. Interestingly, the DEA took all my glass bongs but did not touch a collection of opium pipes that were on my desk, as if to say pot is more dangerous than opium!

Before I could ask any questions or offer up my version of what had happened, Richard went on to tell me that he would be willing to defend me for a retainer of one hundred thousand dollars. I didn't hesitate for a moment. Yes! No problem! I was ready to go to court and fight these bastards! My civil rights and the country's constitutional rights were being trampled and someone had to stand up to these criminals. I mean, how dare these Nazis raid my house in the middle of the night with automatic weapons! They could have just called me and calmly explained how I was breaking the law. They would have saved a lot of time, money, trouble, and resources had they just picked up the phone. I'm not an unreasonable person. I honestly had no idea there was anything illegal about our company. I mean, Chong Glass was in the midst of being audited by the IRS at the time of the raid. Doesn't that say something about being legit?

Paris was especially upset because he had sunk so much of his soul into this glass business that was struggling along, barely surviving. He is such an artist that he would only produce the finest hand-blown glass pipes— pieces that outsold my hand carved pipes by 80 percent at the art gallery. The glass bongs were more than just smoking devices; these were high quality art pieces collected by serious glass art collectors. This fact, among others, was to be part of our defense when and if we appeared in front of a jury.

As I sat in Richard's office that morning, I told the lawyers I resolved to make a stand. I was willing to go to court and fight for the right to exercise my civil rights and my pursuit of happiness, to be free of unreasonable search and seizures. I went on to describe how hemp was once the largest legal cash crop in America and how there had been a law mandating that farmers grow it. I told them that the sails that powered the ships that discovered America were made of hemp and how the word "canvas" was derived from "cannabis." I described how the Chinese used the buds from the plant as medicine to cure a number of ailments, such as menstrual cramps. I described how the logging and timber industry led by the Hearst newspaper company had demonized hemp by printing lies about its effect on "Negros," serving to incite the racist hatred that was common in those days. I even tried to include the bird feed industry and the commercial paint industry that lost a safe and natural product and millions of dollars because of the U.S. government's proracist, pro-chemical company, and prologging company stance.

I tried to educate them on the harm caused by their unconstitutional and cruel laws imposed on a helpless and peaceful culture—laws that only served to show the world how ignorant and behind the times this government is. I told them I would not buckle and compromise my beliefs no matter what.

I was also looking forward to presenting marijuana facts to the public—facts that had been painstakingly researched by different writers, doctors, people in the science community, drug abuse specialists. And they concluded that not only is pot not harmful to people, but that it has valuable use in pain control and has helped countless people with cancer, AIDS, and MS. I had been seeing these reports coming in from all over the world, and I thought that everyone in their right mind would just want to legalize it immediately.

Oh, I went on and on about how could they do this and how could they do that until I noticed that the lawyers were not as fired up as I thought they should be. They just sat there, looking at me very patiently the way a dog looks at the person who feeds him.

Once I was finished with my pot lecture, they proceeded to lay out my options. Yes, we could fight the bastards and we would probably get any jury on my side, but why don't we all go home and think about it for a couple of days while we find out what the government wants. Richard was so kind and understanding and, as he was a friend, I was convinced that he would find a way out of this mess. I was sure that once Richard met with the people who started all this, he would be able to convince them that we were operating a completely legal business and that we did not intend in any way whatsoever to break any laws.

I know that my son was aware of certain places where selling bongs was prohibited, and I knew he took every precaution not to ship to those places. Richard was very reassuring and kind as he escorted us from the law office, but I noticed Mike was not happy at all. In fact, he looked a bit sick.

During the period right after the raid, however, I

was still in denial. I had done nothing wrong, in my mind, so I had nothing to fear . . . or so I thought. I was so sure of my innocence.

I really wanted to find a way to appear in court in front of a jury, where I knew my popularity would hold some weight and where my perspective would at least be heard. But every suggestion I made was met with reality checks. The government held all the cards. I would not be allowed to present any "promarijuana testimony," nor would I be able to show anything other than evidence that related to the charge.

I was under the false impression that nothing would happen to me. I would be treated the same as other pipe manufacturers who had been charged with the same offense and probably sentenced to six months house arrest and one year probation. Well, that sounded pretty good to me. In fact, I was prepared to accept a longer sentence. I looked forward to spending a whole year at home if need be. Two years? Hey, all right! I'll do anything for the cause. My workshop/art studio needed me. My swimming pool needed me. My rooftop garden needed me. I needed a break from the road. It would be perfect.

The lawyers kept discussing my "defense," which totally confused me. What defense? I thought we were going to strike a deal with the prosecution. Well, they said, you need a lawyer in Pittsburgh, where the case is being tried, and you need to embark on a program to "change your image." *Oh yeah, change my image!* Fuck! Who did they think they were dealing with? Cheech? "Hey, man!"

One way was to hire a "celebrity publicist," someone who specialized in getting "good" press. This could be mine for an additional forty thousand dollars. Forty fucking thousand! And that was just the retainer! I was beginning to feel like the drunken slut at a frat party. You know, the one who gets passed around for everyone to fuck. My gut feeling wasn't good. I felt like I was going down.

The truth is, I was never involved in the drug trade. I was merely a spokesman for harmless pot smokers, a comedian who wrote, directed, and acted in what could be described as pro-pot comedy movies. The fact of the matter is, these drug laws, which have been piling up over the years, are so stacked against the accused that the lawyers' role essentially boils down to appearing in court or sending an assistant to stand beside the poor soul when he is sentenced to whatever jail term is predetermined by the courts. And if the defendant has the gall to take the case to trial, he is hit with an automatic enhancement of his sentence. In other words, he is given more jail time just because he tried to defend himself.

Now, that is in direct contrast of what a free society is supposed to be. This is only part of the reason why America has more people incarcerated than any other country. The sad truth is, once you are caught in this system, it is almost impossible to escape from it. But truth will prevail, and everyone engaged in this oppression will have to pay the price . . . eventually.

CHAPTER FOUR

K'an / The Abysmal (Water)
K'an / K'an

Ambition and presumption always lead to danger.

The lawyers eventually traveled to Pittsburgh, where a top local criminal attorney, Stanton Levenson, was also hired to represent me. My lawyers met with the U.S. Attorneys, and we waited patiently until we were finally summoned to hear the "deal." The news was not good! Oh, yes, the U.S. Attorneys knew who I was and what I represented, which was the main reason for Operation Pipe Dreams, the raid that ended up costing the tax-payers a great deal of money—around twelve million dollars, to be exact. The bottom line was they wanted me, plain and simple! They wanted to make an example of the "Pope of Pot," the "Hemp Messiah."

The deal was, either I plead guilty to one count of "conspiring to sell and distribute pot pipes across state lines," or they would charge both my wife and son and we would all go down. *Those dirty bastards!* I thought. *Those dirty rotten bastards! They got me!*

There was no way on Earth I would put my family at risk. And I was particularly concerned about my wife. My son and I were the ones who started the glass business. My wife was merely a cosignatory for the loan that started the business.

But by then I knew how the government operated. They have no qualms about incarcerating innocent people. The government has been doing it for years now. Even during the Clinton administration, Susan McDougal served two years because she would not give false testimony to Ken Starr, the special prosecutor who was conducting the Whitewater investigation. The Republicans were trying to bring Clinton down so they could gain power and, well, the rest is history.

I grew up that day. I finally became a man who realized what a bullshit dream I was living. The America that was founded on that beautiful constitution drafted by the founding fathers no longer existed, if in fact it ever did. The truth had emerged. The dream state ended. The present government had singled me out, along with my hippie culture, and was intent on destroying both of us.

Right after we were raided, I accepted, through my attorneys, a deal from the government. I would plead guilty to one count of sending marijuana pipes through the mail across state lines in exchange for a promise from the government that they would not charge my wife or my son. The penalty for such an offense was a $250,000 fine and up to one year in jail.

I wasn't the least bit worried. I felt there wasn't a judge in America who would sentence me to anything more than probation or maybe house arrest.

Our company was still in the red, despite my popularity. In fact, it was determined that we were a whopping half a million in the hole at the time of the raid. This was due in part to the high labor and parts costs and my son's insistence that we produce only the highest grade of expensive product, staying away from the money-making plastic products that could have generated millions of dollars in profits. We were more of an art studio as opposed to an income-generating factory.

I appeared in Pittsburgh on May 12, 2003, for formal arraignment on the charges and my guilty plea. The judge in my case was supposedly chosen by random selection, but it appeared to me that Bush himself had handpicked him. My lawyers freaked when they were informed which judge we were facing. They called as soon as the judge was chosen and told me, "We are in trouble." I asked how "we" could be in any more trouble than we already were.

Again, I was told that the only chance I had of improving the odds of my appearance in court before this hard-ass judge was to change the stoner image that I had crafted over the years. *Oh, no problem,* I thought.

I'll just go back in time and change the years of recording the albums and the movies and the years of touring. No problem at all!

The lawyers' solution was to obtain letters from all my influential friends, telling the judge what a swell guy I was. They also suggested that I become champion of the antidrug campaign by writing and performing a series of antidrug commercials. Now we were talking! I liked that idea. I really did! I had always thought the antidrug folks were missing the mark by not addressing the real issues, and this would be my chance to get it right.

The absolute worst way to try to convince people not to do something is by harping on whatever it is they're not supposed to do. I had some pretty strong views on how to steer kids away from drugs, including marijuana, which I still do not consider a dangerous drug. It's more like a minor mind-expanding pit stop in one's life that you will or will not experience, depending on whether or not you are a skateboarder.

But the government has a habit of treating pot just the same as they treat heroin. They wanted me to bow my head and admit that I was wrong. They wanted me to grovel and say that pot is the gateway to heroin. That's when I came up with the perfect idea for an antidrug commercial: salsa dancing as an alternative to the stoner lifestyle that I portrayed in the Cheech and Chong movies.

Now, that might sound like a completely stoned idea to you, but I actually thought it would work. The salsa dance itself deters people from indulging in mind-altering substances because of the physical demands of the dance. I know from firsthand experience that I could not smoke pot and dance salsa. It is just impossible to do both at the same time. Salsa dancing is tough to learn and very tough to do straight, let alone high. (I tried it once, but it made me lose my balance.)

Besides, dancing gives you a nicer high. It's a great cardio workout, you don't get the munchies, you dress in nice clothes, and you get to dance with beautiful women. And the better you can dance, the more beautiful the women who will ask you to dance with them. So I decided to make a commercial with Cheech that would show me turning down a chance to smoke up because I would rather dance salsa. It sounds kind of lame now when I see the idea in print . . . but I was gung-ho at the time.

Salsa (or mambo) is such a special dance with an interesting history. It all started in Cuba and South America when the African slaves and the Spanish slaves got together in the cane fields after work. The Africans brought out the drums, while the Spanish brought out the guitars and horns. Together they created the mambo rhythms and melodies. "Mambo," by the way, is an African word that translates as "to tell a story." Mambo became the name of a popular dance that was all the rage in America during the thirties and forties and into the fifties. It evolved into what we now call salsa in the sixties, when a bandleader named Tito Puente would shout out "Salsa!" while playing a hot mambo tune at his gigs.

I learned the dance in 1995 when my gorgeous wife decided she wanted to do something without me. She had reached that stage in her life where she wanted to do some things on her own, so she started taking salsa lessons. I never paid attention because I was busy doing "my thing," which was mainly smoking a lot of pot.

Shelby began going to dances without me, and although she did invite me along, my ego, coupled with my macho-man "dancing is girly" way of thinking, got in the way of wanting to learn to dance. One day, however, my wife invited me to a show where she and her dance instructor were performing salsa for a group of people. I was not prepared for this moment that would prove to be a real turning point in my life.

I never really understood (or cared, for that matter) what exactly salsa dancing was. I thought it was another one of those dumb ballroom dances where the guy twirls his partner around the floor, all the while looking like he has a board stuck up his ass. But I know women like to be twirled, so I was ready for an evening of whirling.

The audience, which consisted mainly of white, middle-aged businessmen, waited patiently while Nester, the dance teacher, set up his sound equipment and prepared the stage. I found a ringside table right next to the stage and sat there sipping a Diet Coke. I felt a twitch of excitement in the pit of my stomach, which usually tells of some impending danger; I looked around for indications of trouble and saw nothing but half-drunk businessmen.

The music started, and I watched as Nester and Shelby approached each other from opposite sides of the stage, looking into one another's eyes. Shelby looked absolutely stunning in her too-short salsa skirt. And Nester looked like a Latin lover, with his dark, brooding, serious "salsero" gaze. The moment was electrifying and silenced the now interested businessmen. The two dancers circled each other while the music throbbed with sexy Latin rhythms. Nester suddenly reached out and grabbed Shelby, holding her close to his body and staring into her eyes.

Every jealous bone in my body began to tremble. The feeling in the pit of my stomach grew into a huge heartache that never really went away. I can feel the pain right now as I write this and remember that night. Nester turned Shelby and they began the dance. They were incredibly smooth as they danced so close, never taking their eyes off of each other throughout the entire dance. They were not just dancing. Hell no! The two of them were making love!

The music shifted into a hypnotic African rhythm, and Nester twirled and whirled Shelby with her head occasionally plunging dangerously close to the floor.

The feelings that coursed through my body that night were strange. They were feelings I had never experienced before. It was as if I was watching the woman I loved fucking some other guy! I was beyond jealous. I was insane.

The dance ended with Nester dipping Shelby in what I was to find out later was called the "big dip." Her feet and beautiful legs were in the air with her head almost touching the ground. The short salsa dress fell toward her head revealing her sexy underwear. That was the final straw.

Fuck this! I thought. *Fuck it! I have to learn this dance.* There is nothing more motivating than watching the woman you adore staring deeply into another man's eyes as he deftly works her body. I vowed to learn that damn dance in record time, convinced that I'd lose my wife if I didn't.

The crowd went nuts, applauding and yelling. Nester took Shelby's hand and they bowed gracefully. Shelby spotted me in the crowd and approached me with a big happy grin on her flushed face.

"Did you like it?" she asked.

"It was amazing!" I answered back in a voice I did not recognize. It wasn't my voice. It was the thin, phony, wimpy voice of a jealous husband confronted by his wife whom he has just walked in on with another man.

"I almost fell! Did you see when I almost fell?" Shelby asked breathlessly.

I mumbled something that made no sense at all, but it didn't matter because she wasn't talking to me. She was talking to Nester, who was now getting all her attention.

"You did great! Didn't she do great?" Nester asked me, while looking at Shelby.

I think it was the way they looked at each other while they danced that pissed me off more than anything else. And I just stood there, rooted to the floor, as they continued looking at each other! Now I really felt invisible. My entire body felt like I had been run over by a truck. Every bone in my body ached. I wanted to run away but I was stuck. I had to face the reality of the situation. I had to learn salsa.

The ride home was very quiet. Shelby sat beside me, silently basking in the glow of a show well done. I had to admit she looked like a pro. All the dance lessons had paid off. If only I had accepted her many invitations to come along, I would not be acting like a jealous asshole.

I had asked her to join me on the road, but she refused until I offered to teach her how to be a stand-up comic. She picked it up quickly and became my opening act in no time. I had to do something besides acting like a fool or risk losing my wife and opening act at the same time. I had to learn the dance.

The next day I called Nester and took my first salsa lesson. It wasn't as easy as it looked—in fact, it was fucking hard. The basic step was hard. Keeping my head up was hard. I threw myself into the effort with a passion I didn't know I had. I even went on a salsa cruise by myself. Nester was with me teaching the class so I felt comfortable. He and I had become good friends, and I practiced incessantly the entire cruise. I even stayed on the boat when it docked in Mexico, dancing with anyone who would dance with me. I had brought a portable, battery-operated boom box so I could set up shop anywhere. I was almost insane with the need to learn this fucking dance. Nester and I stayed up until four in the morning, dancing and talking about salsa almost every night, until we docked at San Pedro, California, near Long Beach.

Most of the tour people were from Vancouver. However, I was living in Los Angeles, an hour drive from the port. I had come alone and I was one of the first to leave the ship. This is where the cruise could have had a sad ending. I had totally forgotten that we had to go through U.S. customs and immigration since we had gone to Mexico. And I wasn't prepared when the customs inspector called me out of the line and asked me to open my bag. This is when I remembered bringing a small bag of pot (for which I had a medical prescription) and an expensive silver inlayed pot pipe. I brought the stash thinking I was going to have a couple of after-hour tokes to celebrate my learning the dance. However, since I didn't quite accomplish that mission,

I totally forgot about the pot, and now I was seconds away from a bad scene.

The inspector started asking me questions while she rummaged through the bag. The pot and the pipe were in the side pocket. I could see the bulge of both items.

When the agent asked me where I lived, I used the question as an opportunity to let her know who I was, hoping she was a fan and would be a little more understanding when she came across the pot.

"Yeah, I'm doing some research for a movie about a cruise ship," I lied.

"Will this be a Cheech and Chong movie?" she asked while she zipped up the bag. Her hand now rested on the pot.

I began to sweat but answered in a calm voice, "Uh, yeah! It will be a Cheech and Chong movie. Yeah!"

"Well, I'll go see it," she replied, as she handed back my bag. "I love Cheech and Chong."

I walked off the boat and into a waiting cab, trying my best not to run. I could not believe she did not feel the pot. Her hand was right on the stash. I dodged another bullet. *Wow!* I thought. *I am so fucking blessed.*

But that was back in 1995. In 2003 I faced criminal indictment and was awaiting sentencing after entering a plea.

My defense lawyers had turned me over to another attorney in their office to more or less babysit me until my sentencing date. Shelia, who was a tall, attractive, ex-hippie lawyer with a sixties social conscience, was outraged at what had happened to me. We hit it off immediately and had several sessions where we discussed different ways of showing the court what a swell guy I really was. My gut reaction was that this approach was a big waste of time, but I went along with the recommendation and worked with Shelia on my letter-writing campaign. I did enjoy talking to her, and she seemed genuinely interested in hearing about my life, so we spent many enjoyable afternoons talking about the early days, while trying to keep my ass out of jail.

Well, we got letters from all of my friends. Nice letters, telling the judge what a nice guy I was. I even managed to get a letter from Patti Davis, Ronald Reagan's daughter. However, it was too brief to be of any value except to mention it in this book. It went something like, "I know Tommy Chong from World Gym. Signed, Patti Davis." That was the whole letter! I think I kept it somewhere. It's classic!

Something told me that collecting all these letters of recommendation was a big waste of time, but my attorneys felt it was a good idea. Deep down, I knew I was going to jail. Not for the crime itself, but for all the movies I had made with Cheech that were still being played regularly, creating yet another generation of Cheech and Chong fans. I was a threat to the current right-wing government and I had to be removed from the scene. Nobody can beat the Feds. Not me, not Martha Stewart, nobody! But I also know that nobody beats the Truth. Not me and certainly not the Feds. Remember Nixon?

The signs were there. Everywhere I looked I was reminded of where I was headed. I would watch the movie *The Shawshank Redemption* over and over, and any live show about the prison system would keep me in front of the television set for hours. But my fascination with prisons started when I was in my teens, back in Calgary, Alberta, Canada.

I was sixteen, and I was a rebel. I met a couple of ex-convicts at a pool hall where I hung out, and even brought some home to live with my family. My mother was very cool, and as long as they paid rent and respected our family, she could care less that they had been in jail. I think she had that understanding attitude because my aunt had served some prison time—a fact that was never mentioned except for the occasional evening when my aunt would get drunk and start telling stories. One of my ex-convict roommates gave me a biker tattoo on my upper right arm when I was fifteen years old. It was a homemade job done with a needle and black India ink. Neither of my parents objected to the tat, just to give you an idea of how cool they were.

McCann, the biker, used to tell me stories of his time in jail. He did his time in the midfifties in a jail where the silent system was in effect. The silent system was brutal! The inmates were not allowed to talk unless given permission by the guards, and anyone caught talking would be punished. They would be tied to a cell and beaten with a wooden paddle so big it had to be held with two hands. And that was just the punishment for talking!

McCann learned to sing in a whisper so that no one could hear him. The longest sentence at that penitentiary was two years, but two years is a long time to go without talking. He told me enough horror stories that I swore I'd never go to jail. I think his stories did more to keep me out of trouble than anything else.

When McCann moved out, I met another newly released prisoner from Montreal, Quebec, named "Frenchy." Gilles Frechette was his real name, and he introduced me to show business. He was a great tap dancer and loved to dance whenever he could. Gilles wasn't that tall—I guess about five feet five and about 130 pounds—but he could tap up a storm. I would bring him to parties and he would become the entertainment. He would bring his tap music and make his entrance, adapting his performance to the layout of the house. Sometimes he would tap his way down the stairs or from the kitchen. All my friends loved his little tap show almost as much as Gilles.

He was the first con I knew who got homesick for prison! He told me how he and some of the other prisoners would perform for the other cons at the prison Christmas show, how they prepared three months ahead, making costumes and planning the various numbers. I could see he was tormented by the fact that he was going to miss the show that year.

Gilles worked as a waiter in a coffee shop for a while, then he got a job delivering prescription eyeglasses to the retail shops, but he wasn't happy. He tried to go straight in so many ways, but his love of the beloved prison Christmas show got the best of him, and one day just before Christmas, Gilles dressed up like a woman and robbed a bank. The cops arrested him the next day and recovered almost all of the money. The amount missing totaled the exact sum Gilles owed my mother for rent. She attended his trial and waved goodbye as the happy Frenchman made it back to jail in time to do the Christmas show.

The closest I came to jail as a teenager was the night my friends and I had a very close brush with death. The night started out normal and quiet, considering our ages and our quest for excitement. I think we went to a dance, although I really don't remember that part. I do remember sitting at a table in a restaurant in Chinatown with a couple of friends of mine from school. They were brothers and cousins who played football with my older brother, Stan. We were actually more like acquaintances than close friends, so when my friend showed up dangling car keys, my acquaintances had no idea the car they were about to be riding in was stolen.

I knew because stealing, or rather "borrowing,"

cars and riding them around town was the thing to do in those days. One of the car thieves got so brazen he actually kept a couple of the nicer cars for himself, driving them to and from school like he owned them. The usual MO was to drive the shit out of them and leave them within walking distance of your house. We were out of control and it would be just a matter of time before we got caught.

My jock friends, who thought they were just getting a ride home, jumped in the stolen car and away we went. My car-thief friend was part Indian and part white man and was very good-looking with dark blue eyes. He looked like the typical badass in town and had the most demonic laugh whenever he did something crazy. He drove through town and out on a country road going faster and faster while the jocks were shitting their pants in fear. I was riding shotgun and clutching the armrest with both hands. None of us was wearing a seat belt because the car, which was a 1950 Plymouth, didn't have any. The car slid back and forth on the gravel road as my friend drove faster and faster, laughing his crazy laugh.

Then suddenly the car left the road and sailed into a slough, turning over onto its roof. The water cushioned the crash and saved our lives. The fact that we weren't wearing seat belts also saved us from drowning in the almost four-feet-deep water. The only injury suffered by any of us was a deep gash in the thumb of the jock in the backseat. He cut himself climbing out of the broken window.

The accident happened on a deserted part of the road, so we had to walk to a darkened house. The door was open, so we went in and tried to find a light, but it appeared that the place was a bunkhouse for the farm workers and was without electricity. We made our way back to the road and flagged down a car. The driver had seen the wreckage and was glad to see we all survived. He gave us a ride right to our respective houses and dropped off the injured jock at the local hospital, where he had his thumb stitched up and was questioned by a couple of detectives.

The same detectives paid me a visit at my job the next day and asked me what had happened. I told them what I knew, and when they asked me who was driving, I tried to pretend I didn't know the guy that well. But Calgary is a small town, and the cops knew who he was when they first got the call from the hospital. My friend was sentenced to two years in the pen—two years for stealing a car! That seemed like a long time back then, but now you can get twenty years here in the States for a lesser crime if you have pot or a gun in the car.

I felt like I had betrayed my friend, so I tried to beat up the jocks that told on him. That was a waste of time, because, even though they were afraid of me, they were jocks. They were bigger and stronger, and the only one

I could have maybe beaten up had left town. I met him at a gym years later and he told me I was responsible for him leaving town and becoming a respected art dealer in London. It's nice to know my delinquency helped at least one person!

CHAPTER FIVE

Ting / The Caldron

Li / Sun

Acceptance of one's fate, and of being guided.

In the period between the bust and my sentencing, Shelia was my one bright spot at the law firm. She introduced me to the president of Volunteers of America, the organization that does the Head Start program for underprivileged children who need help in schools. In turn, they put me in touch with the people at a ghetto school named A Place Called Home. The privately funded school is located in the heart of the ghetto and helps the local kids by giving them the opportunity for a good education. I was so impressed with the founder and her staff that I immediately volunteered my money and my services.

Volunteers of America put me to work teaching a theater class with their summer program at a college in the City of Orange right next to Disneyland. It was my very first teaching gig and I loved every moment of it. Teaching is a lot like doing stand-up comedy, except you have much more control over the audience. Well, in theory, that is. The ghetto kids in my class were preparing to attend high school, so I had the brightest and the best in my class. But they were also the savviest. These kids had seen much more of real life than most adults. Growing up in the gang-infested poor part of the city, kids develop survival skills that can appear to be an uncaring and unloving demeanor to the unsuspecting adult. However, when they find out that you are as hip and real as they are, that's when the fun begins.

A few of the kids knew who I was and they soon let the others know who was teaching the TV theater class. Soon my class was packed to capacity. I even had a few teachers from the other classes sit in a few times. Thankfully, I had given this volunteer job a lot of thought before teaching my first class. I knew from my experience with my own children how tough it could be to keep their attention. The class had to be different, yet not too weird or too theaterlike.

This was not an easy assignment, because, like stand-up comedy, you have about five minutes to make an impression—to set the tone, so to speak. Then you have an hour and a half to keep them enthralled and interested in what you are trying to teach them. And unlike acting classes, where people pay to be yelled at, you have to be very careful with the discipline trip.

The kids had to be controlled or else they would control me, but I couldn't slap the shit out of them or even yell at them. This was going to be a challenge. *Wow,* I thought. *What was I thinking? Why did I allow my self to say yes to this gig? Did I really need to do this?*

All these thoughts and more were rushing through my brain as I drove to my first class. It took me a good hour to get there, so I had plenty of time to ask myself why over and over again. But as soon as I arrived on campus, a gentle calm came over me and I knew not only that everything would work out, but that I was going to have fun. As soon as I saw the kids I was going to be teaching, I felt very calm and ready.

Junior high school kids—this was my favorite age group and the one that I never really grew out of. Each day is a new adventure to these kids, especially with the opposite sex. This is the age where you notice the differences between boys and girls, the age when the littlest thing can become a big drama, when "nobody understands you." Hell, *you* don't understand you! You are growing so fast, you really don't feel comfortable with your body. The girls sprout breasts overnight, while the guys start feeling sexual feelings over just about anything.

I remember going to sleep with a high squeaky voice and waking up with a low baritone and a perpetual hard-on. My mother thought there was someone else in the house. Kids at that age are confused and disorientated for good reason, so when they are confronted with unfeeling adults, their problems just seem to multiply. I had an advantage in the classroom because I still remember the feeling like it was yesterday. This is why Cheech and I have always been so popular with teenagers. We relate to them.

The greatest feeling when you become a teenager is the first taste of freedom. You have become a person. You are no longer just a son or a daughter, but a person. You get to sit at the big table at some of the family gatherings. You now have private thoughts, and this can be very disturbing to parents because they used to always know where you were and what you were thinking, but now it's a new ball game.

I remember when I hit fifteen. My father, who really loved me, couldn't stand me. He hated everything about me: the way I dressed, the way I walked, the way I talked, and the people I hung out with. He refused to even talk to me for months. I totally understood and actually enjoyed the conflict because he never got physical with me—except one time, when I told him I was quitting school. He wanted to know why, and when I told him, he didn't like my tone of voice and he slapped me so hard I ended up upside down in a closet! It was the only time in my life that he hit me, and I was so impressed with the power and the speed of the slap.

Pop was only five foot three, but he had been a top athlete in school, and being Chinese in Canada in the twenties, he knew how to fight. I was just thankful that he used an open hand. Who knows what I would have looked like had he hit me with a fist! But I deserved it. Had I been in his shoes I would have smacked me too. I was obnoxious and I thought I was bad, as in outlaw bad.

My friends, who were a group of wannabe hoods and high school dropouts, picked fights with local athletes and soldiers wherever we went. This was after drinking all the alcohol we could lay our hands on. I had a job that paid very little, but it was more than most of my slacker friends had. And it was party time every weekend without fail. The one thing that kept me out of jail was my ability to listen to my gut. And the times I failed to listen to the "voice," I would pay—like the night I did finally go to jail.

My best friend, Ronnie, had stolen a car and came over to my house to pick me up. Now, this was right after my other friend had been sentenced to jail. So did I learn from the car crash? No, not even a little. The ironic thing about this episode was that we never got the car running; we never committed the crime we were eventually accused of committing, which was joyriding. Why? Because the fucking car never ran! It died on my friend when he came to pick me up. He had to walk over to my house to get me to help him start the fucking thing.

We were under the hood, leaning into the motor trying to figure out what was wrong, when a patrol car drove up behind us. Apparently, they thought we were having car trouble and were stopping to help. But of course we took one look at them and ran like the idiots we were, making it into my house and jumping into bed with our clothes on. We tried to fake like we'd been there all night, but we were arrested about five minutes later by the police, who just followed our tracks in the newly fallen snow.

I loved the way my mother tried to say we had been home all night. She would lie like crazy for me, and then beat my ass purple when she got me home. This time her lies didn't help us; we were caught. Of course, we both spilled our guts when the cops asked us what was going on, ruining whatever hope our lawyer had of getting us off. They took us to the city jail that was located in the basement of the city hall building and locked us in the communal drunk tank.

My father bailed us out the next day and we eventually pleaded guilty to joyriding in a stolen car and were fined one hundred dollars. But one night seemed like an eternity then. I thought I had learned a lesson I'd never forget, but I guess we never stop learning. My father paid the fine, but he never yelled at me or got down on me. In fact, he did the opposite. He had his friend Jerry, a fellow trucker and drinking partner, talk to me. Jerry had been in and out of jail a couple of times, so he knew the signs. He saw the potential criminal in me and nipped it in the bud in a very simple but effective way.

He gave me fifty dollars and the keys to his car and told me, "Whenever you need a car or money, you don't have to steal. Just come to me and I'll give you mine." And that was that. No lectures, no threats. It was just a simple gesture of faith and love from a man who'd been down that road.

My father was also very cool about my wild side, and although he hated how I dressed and how I looked, he never stopped giving me love. He also kept me from a life of joyriding by being available to pick me up from parties or wherever I was regardless of the time. I knew I could phone him night or day and he'd come and get me. The only payback he wanted was the promise that when I had kids, I'd do the same for them. And I kept that promise as best I could. I was very lucky having a father and mother who were that cool.

The only drawback was my friends and my brother's friends all treated my parents like they were their parents. Ex-girlfriends would come by to visit my parents because they became so close to them. They were through with me, but they stayed friends with Mom and Pop right up until my parents both passed away.

So there I was, teaching kids theater, but really I was just teaching them what to look for when they grew into adults—another full circle.

The first thing I wanted to teach the kids was meditation. Meditation has been around for thousands of years. Some religions base their entire philosophy around the practice, and some religions use meditation as a religion.

Cheech was the first person to introduce me to meditation. He was on to the same trip as the Beatles for a while, which was Transcendental Meditation, introduced by Let Me Ram Yerbum, the gay guru. When I saw him meditate for the first time, I thought he was just taking a nap. But I found out many years later just how powerful and effective meditation is, and it has changed my entire outlook on life.

I learned it by reading a book called *The Art of Meditation* by Joel Goldsmith. The one difference between Joel's style of meditation and that of the Buddhist tradition is that Joel brings God into the experiences, whereas the Buddhist style is more about the individual—God is not mentioned. I personally like the Joel Goldsmith method because I like knowing that when I meditate, there is an outside chance that God might talk to me personally. I have had messages from the Holy Spirit from time to time, and it has been wonderful . . . actually, beyond wonderful. There is such a great feeling of calmness when that happens. It is peace beyond understanding.

I never got too much into the God trip when I taught my class because I didn't want to turn the kids off and because religion is so personal that it is hard not to offend someone when you teach religion. It falls into the category of "ask and ye shall receive," and if they don't ask, you certainly don't push it on them. The kids responded favorably to the meditation, I think, because it allowed them a few moments to get into themselves and because meditation is so refreshing. It's like taking a nap in the middle of the day.

The first time we did the meditation there were a few in the class who thought it was stupid and had a hard time falling into it. But that lasted only minutes and in no time at all the entire class had their eyes closed and were deep into meditation. I used a bit of that time to remind the kids how special they all were. I know from experience that we all have to be reminded constantly how great we all are so that we will act great. Kids really need to be reminded constantly because they are changing so rapidly. After reminding them how wonderful each and every one of them was, I broke the meditation and proceeded to teach the class. It was great having a class full of quiet attentive kids waiting for the next trip.

I lectured about the art of acting for a few minutes, telling them how acting plays such a major roll in our lives every single day because there is rarely a time when we are not interacting with others. You act when you talk to your parents, especially when you want something— and when you are a teenager you are in constant need. You act when you talk to your teachers, your coaches, and your friends. Some of you become comedians when you are with your friends because you have someone to laugh with. And even the loners act. They act like they like being alone, and I believe they do, because if they didn't they would have friends. So acting is living, and before you can learn how to act, you must learn the best way to live. And because no two people are the same, acting then becomes a personal activity.

Now, the most important secret to acting—and there are many secrets—is revealed only to those who seek out the secret. When I taught the summer class, I had kids who really wanted to learn and I had kids who could care less about any old secret. The one thing they did have in common was that they were there in the class, so they were all going to learn about the secret regardless of attitude. Oh, we had a fun time that summer! I loved teaching because a teacher learns so much while teaching. It is like a cook who gets to eat what he or she cooks.

The secret of acting, by the way, is being aware of when you are acting and when you are just being. Being is when you are doing something or reacting to someone in a pure, natural manner. When you become aware of the difference, then you know the secret. Of course, the real school of acting is real life, which is why most acting teachers will tell their students that only time will make them actors. Putting kids on that first step of their journey is so rewarding and exciting.

I would arrive an hour early to prepare the classroom and sit in meditation as I waited, completely in my element. Once they arrived, I would lecture for a while and then I would turn on a salsa tape and teach salsa. Now that was fun! The kids' reactions varied along predictable lines. There were the ones who knew how to salsa and there were the ones who not only didn't know, but did not want to learn. I never pressured anyone, but I did encourage them all to try in a gentle manner. Some jumped right in and some of them watched for a couple of classes before they tried it. But in the end everyone was doing it.

The summer was quickly coming to a close and my teaching assignment was also ending. The kids were amazing, as kids can be. There were a few dropouts, but the bulk of the class learned how to meditate and a few learned how to salsa. During the last class they performed a skit that they wrote themselves for the rest of the school. The fact that they did it by themselves showed me that I had accomplished my mission. It made me feel really good.

CHAPTER SIX

Chên / The Arousing (Shock, Thunder)
Chên / Chên

*Despite the rumblings of shock, we should
keep our attitude neutral and disengaged.*

September 11, 2003, my sentencing date, was fast
approaching, and I was performing almost every weekend with Shelby at comedy clubs across the country,
working two shows a night for my adoring fans. The
news accounts of my bust had the clubs packed with
people who wanted to see the old stoner one more time
before he went to jail.

Despite the nightmare of this whole ordeal, at least
the bong bust provided us with some badly needed
material. Our show had gotten quite predictable, and
the new material gave us new energy and a new point of
view. As always, the fans were very generous with their
stash, but I felt too energized to smoke. I was on a natural high, buzzed out of my mind with indignation.

The truth is, I never smoked as much pot as my loyal fans thought I did, which is one of the reasons the DEA found so much pot at my house. People all over the country would give me their best buds that I would then "donate" to my pot-smoking friends and to the opening acts at the various clubs and venues. I would also go on periodic pot fasts when I wouldn't smoke at all. The day of the raid I started a "protest fast" that I am still on today. I vowed that day that I would only smoke pot when it was legal.

The authorities, however, thought the stoner character I played in the movies was the real me. I was still in denial about the whole ordeal. I felt I was only going to receive house arrest. I mean, how could they put me in jail for a bong? It did not compute. But deep down inside I knew better, and I know my lawyers also knew better.

The time of reckoning finally arrived and we flew into Pittsburgh for my September 11 court date. It was surreal landing at the airport and being asked for autographs by fans on the eve of my sentencing. I had been in Pittsburgh many times before with Cheech and we were treated like rock stars, so except for the different nature of this particular gig, everything else seemed somewhat normal.

The rest of my family had arrived and was waiting at the hotel, where I was greeted by even more autograph seekers. The press had been notified, and we had to enter the hotel from the side entrance to escape the photographers—a move that was completely contrary to my nature. I have always enjoyed the paparazzi. The tabloids never use pictures of me so I have nothing to fear. The tabloids feed off of the Paris Hiltons of the world, not off the Chong family.

My wife, my son, and I arranged to stay in the same room so we would be together on the last night. The team of lawyers came to our suite that evening to go over the game plan. The mood was somber, depressing, down, but I still felt hope. I could not see how any judge could, in good faith, sentence me to jail for selling bongs. I just could not grasp the logic. But then again I could not grasp the logic of invading Iraq even if they did have weapons of mass destruction.

I actually did a radio interview right after the bust during which I said, "The only weapons of mass destruction found so far were my bongs." This was the truth. However, the Feds were looking for any reason to jump all over me, and I gave them one. Am I sorry I said that? Hell no! I'm a comedian—I'm supposed to say shit like that. Besides, this is America. Many wars have been fought for freedom of speech, and I will never disrespect the oath I took when I became an American citizen to obey and honor the Constitution of the United States.

This current bunch of thieves who are in power now won't be there forever. Their misguided greedy policies cannot withstand the will of the people. They will be voted out or impeached like others before them and we will have our country back.

I, along with many Americans from the sixties, still remember the horrors of the Vietnam conflict, so I could not for the life of me see the logic of sinking into another (unwinnable) war. And the fact that they actually had the time and energy to worry about the water pipe business while making a global mess just didn't make sense. Of course, this was a political move designed to distract the people of America from the real problems. This is why the day of sentencing was set for the infamous September 11.

Our meeting with the legal team went rather smoothly as they tried to prepare me for the worst. Mike was upset that the press had reported that I was facing up to two years and a $250,000 fine. He said he felt like withdrawing the guilty plea. That woke me up!

Yes, we should withdraw the plea and fight these bastards! I was ready to do battle, until Stanton, our Pittsburgh lawyer, reminded me that we would be back where we started, defending Paris and Shelby from getting prison time along with me.

I didn't sleep a wink that night. I lay awake trying to imagine what the next day was going to bring. And I was fed up with the whole system, which all seemed to be a money tree for the lawyers—a money tree fed in part by the notion "if we lose, we will get them on appeal." It is so disgusting how the system has been perverted. The conviction rate for the Feds is somewhere around 100 percent—98.6 percent if you factor in the cases the Feds decide to drop. The system is a joke and a sham. This is the same system that has created the climate for the various revolutions the world has been involved in over the centuries.

The next real revolution will not be the least bit violent. I feel that the Spirit will be involved, and love, peace, and understanding will melt the opposition like ice in warm water. The gentle smile of the child will persuade the oppressor to give up their ways and join the swelling ranks of peace-loving folks as we laugh our way into the future. Death will claim those who threaten the future of this planet because the will to survive will win over the need to suppress. Fear will disappear into the empty void of ignorance and the light of understanding will fill the hearts of all who survive. This was the message that I received the night before the sentencing.

I was wide awake long before the wake-up call came. I had written a statement that I was going to say at the sentencing. I showed it to the lawyers, who read it in silence, and then advised me not to read it in court. They both felt the statement I had prepared—one that actually disowned my past image and blamed my marijuana smoking for my present problems—would be laughed at and ridiculed by the press. And to top it off, the court would still give me jail time. I was relieved not to have to read the statement aloud because it simply was not true. It was what I thought the court wanted to hear.

It was a pleasant fall day and the walk to the courthouse would have been a nice one if not for the somber occasion. I felt a very strange vibe that morning, with me getting happier the closer we got. When we got to the courthouse, we were met by a bevy of reporters shouting questions at me. I heeded my lawyer's advice and said nothing. We made it through the metal detectors and caught the elevator going up.

We were only in the courtroom a few minutes when the judge made his entrance. "All rise. This court is now in session, the honorable Judge Arthur Schwab presiding. . . ." I tried to follow the bailiff's words, but all I could hear were the words "Thy will be done," over and over. "Thy will be done." What was about to happen to me was something that was meant to happen for a reason. This was the message I received while the judge and the lead prosecutor presented their case to the press. At least that's what it felt like—like this was a *Twilight Zone* version of a court of law, wherein my future was decided long before I ever set foot in the courtroom.

My lawyers made a case as to why I should not get jail time. This seemed, at least in part, designed to create a record should I decide to appeal the sentence. The judge barely acknowledged my lawyers, but he did get excited when he was informed that I was willing to make a statement. I had the feeling that he thought I would be so stoned that I would not be able to stand up, let alone talk. But I am a comedian and an audience is an audience, even if it's in a courtroom.

I stood and tried to explain the difference between who I really am and my movie persona. I also went on to tell him that I was sorry for the "crime" that I committed and if given a chance I would start a program designed to keep kids off drugs. This groveling was not hard for me because I am an actor, and playing the defendant was just another role to me.

However, the judge didn't buy my performance one bit. In fact, I think I pissed him off, talking about how I knew that salsa dancing was the answer to the drug problems the world was facing. You could tell he was definitely not the type of man who would go salsa dancing. He probably thought it was some kind of gang slang, some signal to a terrorist group to attack America. Or maybe he thought I was doing a bit and making a mockery of his courtroom when, in fact, I was sincere. Who knows and who really cares what he was thinking. Everyone is entitled to their opinion, and like the muse said, "Thy will be done."

I sat down after my speech and was told to rise for sentencing. Wow, that was fast! I guess the proceedings were cutting into the lunch hour, because the judge suddenly sped everything up. And the words that I imagined him saying in a voice like a record playing on the wrong speed rang through my head.

Mr. Chong, is it not true that you actually put your own wife in your movies? And, Mr. Chong, is it not a fact that you referred to your former partner as "beaner"? Well, it appears I have no other option than to sentence you to nine months in a federal prison. May God have mercy on your butt!

Nine months! I heard my family sigh in defeat. "Thy will be done." Nine months and it would be over. I somehow felt relieved. Nine months. I felt like a pregnant woman. My wife and family came to where I was still standing and we all hugged briefly. I saw the arresting officer and I said quietly, "'Nothing will happen to you'?" repeating the words he had used to get me talking the day they raided my house.

He looked sheepish and mumbled something like, "I can't speak for the judge." The female prosecutor said something about a halfway house. They were all trying to justify the harsh sentence, but all they did was embarrass themselves further. This whole thing was a publicity stunt for the Bush people to distract the press from his botched war in Iraq. His "weapons of mass destruction" turned into "lies of huge proportions." Oh well! "Thy will be done. Forgive them, Father, for they know not what they do."

I was in shock but feeling good. The Presence was with me that day and has been with me ever since. The calm "everything will be all right" feeling stayed with me while we walked back to Stanton's office. It was over, but the lawyers wanted to do a post mortem and talk about the "injustice" of it all.

Stanton, obviously frustrated by the outcome, suggested that only lawyers stand to gain with this system. I think Stanton was right. I admire his candor, and I have the highest regard for his ability and his counsel. I also appreciate the position that Mike and Richard were in as criminal lawyers just doing what they do for their clients. However, I felt betrayed by the whole experience. And as someone who makes a living in Hollywood, I know about betrayal.

I was sentenced and released on my own recognizance (without bail) to the relief of my learned attorneys. I could have been handcuffed and led off immediately to start my sentence, but I guess the court felt they had pushed the line far enough. I still felt like it wasn't over.

"How about an appeal?" I asked. Surely all the judges in Pittsburgh are not as right wing as my judge. Shelby felt the same as I did. Let's appeal! Reluctantly, after a "don't get your hopes up too high" talk, Stanton hooked us up with a Pittsburgh appeals lawyer, who tried to assure us that "of course, we have a chance." Never give up—and the meter keeps running on the lawyer tab.

Finally, a top criminal lawyer in Los Angeles, who lives in our neighborhood, gave us the best advice: to put this whole ordeal behind us. He told me to do the time, then appeal, or do whatever I could do to set things right after I got out of jail. But right now, I should forget the appeal and do the nine months to get it over with. If I were to appeal it would be another nine months before they ever heard the appeal, and if I lost then, I'd still have to go in.

My neighbor went on. "Hey, you're up against the U.S. government. These are the same people who invaded Iraq and Afghanistan just because they could. And who was going to stop them? Let's face it. You don't have a chance. Do the time."

Finally, a straight answer! Actually, I had the answer when I pled guilty to something that is clearly not a crime. "Thy will be done." This had to happen because it brought the issue to court. Although I was prohibited from making any pro-pot commentary at the trial, I certainly had good reason to prove to the court how this government uses their illegal drug laws to incarcerate millions of citizens, ruin countless lives, and spend billions of taxpayer dollars on what is a criminal enterprise of its own. Hopefully, this book will help the poor souls who are presently locked away from their families because of a natural, nonaddictive substance that has been proven to have great medical value to willing adult customers. Oh yes, "thy will be done."

I felt like I was in *Alice in Wonderland*. The bust did feel like an acid trip when I think of it. It was weird. Had I been doing anything illegal, I'm quite sure I would have demanded a lawyer, and I know I would have shut the fuck up. But I knew I wasn't doing anything but being who I've been for the past forty years now. So I did learn an important lesson that morning. Keep your mouth shut no matter what they tell you and demand to see a lawyer. I know if I had said nothing until I had a lawyer I probably would not have done time. The Feds never even had a proper search warrant the morning of the raid. They told me I couldn't have a lawyer until they said so, and I wasn't even involved in the day-to-day of the glass company—another legal matter they conveniently overlooked while they ransacked my house and took all my cash. And the cash they took had nothing to do with the charge I pled guilty to. It really did feel like a movie, a Nazi movie, and I felt like a victim.

The universe has a way of correcting itself, so no matter what happens all we know is that it was supposed to happen. I think the reason the Bush crew got into office was because of us not appreciating President Clinton when we had all those years of peace and prosperity. We became complacent and took peace for granted. And now we have paid the price. I remember when Vietnam ended and everyone said they would never forget the lessons we learned in that war. How soon we forget. And for what? To protect the greedy handful of old men who control big environment-polluting businesses who need a puppet like Bush to continue raping the country?

CHAPTER SEVEN

Chieh / Limitation
K'an / Tui

Acceptance of limits.

We performed our last gig in Muskegon, Michigan, to a sold-out audience. Many of the fans in attendance had themselves served time in jail and were there to give me a proper send-off. There were more than a few prison guards there as well. They also gave me advice and encouragement. One of the fans told me not to worry about drugs in prison. He said, and I quote, "Hell, there's more dope in prison than on the street. I know some guys who bring it in." He was very drunk and loud, but he fit right in with the rest of the crowd.

After we played the gig in Muskegon, we flew home to prepare for my nine months of incarceration. A friend of mine who had just completed two years in the state pen called and told me I could bring in my computer, my guitar, and a television set with earphones. Of

My father, Stan Chong, performing in his mother's theater group, 1914

My brother, Stan; Pop; and me; fishing in Calgary

The Chong family home, a wartime house built for World War II veterans, Calgary Alta, Canada, 1949–56

Crescent Heights High School, Calgary, Canada. I attended during my sophomore and junior years in 1955–57.

My mother, Jean, with my daughter Precious in Stone Canyon, Bel-Air, California, 1980

Three generations of Chong: Paris, me, and Pop in Amsterdam, Holland

I signed with Berry Gordy at Motown in 1967 and wrote and performed "Does Your Mama Know About Me" (a hit song later recorded by Diana Ross) with my band Bobby Taylor & The Vancouvers. The band broke up in 1968, but in 1969 I met Cheech Marin and formed Cheech and Chong.

Daughters Robbi and Rae Dawn, 1984

BOBBY TAYLOR & THE VANCOUVERS
Gordy Recording Artists

photo: Michael Ochs Archives.com

Pop and Paris,
Bel-Air, California, 1979

A movie still from *Far Out Man*, 1988

Promotional sticker from
Cheech and Chong's heyday

Photograph taken from our live act
"Old Man in the Park," 1975, a bit we
stole from the "Committee (San
Francisco)" that was was in turn
stolen from us by the TV producer
Jimmy Komac and became *Chico and
the Man* with Freddie Prinze

Geraldo, Cheech, and me. Taken in 1985, this was the last picture of us together before Cheech and Chong broke up.

Chong Glass. "Thank you for your business."

Got a light?

Me and my bestsellin' "incense burner"

My wife, Shelby, and me, 2002

Chong and the Family Stoned Band, 2001

Me and my homies in Taft Prison

My bodyguard! Samoan High Chief Big Ben, who was my protector in the joint

Shelby and me and her favorite green dress

a/k/a Tommy Chong
documentary photo, 2002

The "Cheech" bong

Me on the roof of my home
testing "product"

course, I believed him. And this was coming from my ex-accountant, who did time for stealing money. I am so gullible I'd believe Charlie Manson if he said he was innocent.

My son convinced me to telephone the prison myself to find out what I would be allowed to bring in with me, and to my great disappointment, I was informed that I would be allowed one pair of white or black running shoes with no logos, a pair of gray sweatpants, a couple of white T-shirts, white socks, a wedding ring, a cheap watch (under fifty dollars in value), and one soft covered religious book of my choosing.

He went on to tell me that although I was due to report in at two o'clock in the afternoon, it would be to my advantage to be there before noon and not a minute later. My friend Josh Gilbert and I drove to the army and navy store in Santa Monica to purchase my new duds, where I was waited on by a homie who knew where I was going based solely on what I was buying. There is quite a jail culture in America now, thanks to the fucked-up laws that have been passed in the last ten years.

As I was leaving, the store clerk wished me luck at Taft. The truth was, up until that point, I hadn't allowed myself to even think of jail. I was *still* blissfully in denial. But the time was approaching when reality would wake me up from the dream and I would be incarcerated for nine months for selling water pipes over the Internet. I knew that I was really going to jail because of the movies we had made in the early eighties. *Up in Smoke, Nice Dreams, Cheech and Chong's Next Movie, The Corsican Brothers,* and *Still Smoking* are still being played regularly on television today. This apparently really pissed off the Bush administration, and they came after my glass water pipe business.

But in my heart, I knew I was going to go to jail because I was told by a small still voice that this was going to happen. When I say "voice," I mean God. I have always had a special relationship with God, as long as I can remember. I know that I have always been drawn to the spiritual side of almost every experience, even when I was a kid. I remember very clearly the feeling of something else around me, guiding me, protecting me.

My early experiences in church were profound and comforting. I remember walking in the snow at night feeling the quiet beauty all around me, wondering if I would see God with my eyes, because I could certainly feel Him with my heart. These quiet moments alone gave me an assurance that I was not alone. I was surrounded with love. I was protected with the love that passes understanding. It is the love of the universe, the love of God, that protects us all when we realize that it exists. This is the "key to heaven" that is mentioned in the Bible and other holy books. It is the knowledge and faith that the Higher Power exists. In a way, it's like knowing the mountaintop exists even though it is obscured by clouds. The Truth that will set you free is simply the knowledge that not only does God exist, He exists within you. God is the very life of your existence. And you can have the Kingdom only if you recognize It.

It shall be according to your faith; in other words, you make your own reality according to what you believe in. If you believe in the devil (I don't) then you will manifest evil (error.) On the contrary, if you believe in love (which I do), then you will manifest love (reality).

It is also almost impossible to commit a crime when you know that God is the essence of your life. Knowing why it is wrong to steal will keep you from becoming a thief. Now, I realize that some of you readers are thinking, *This guy has been smoking too much pot*, which is true. I did smoke way too much pot, and that took my mind off my path and put me in jail, where I got back on my path.

But one cannot blame one's inability to move forward because of smoking too much pot. There are times when even the most dedicated potheads must stop smoking if for no other reason than to enjoy smoking more when they resume. Ineptness or serial procrastination should not be blamed on the hemp plant because the plant itself is not addictive. The only thing pot smokers get addicted to is the effect of feeling good. However, feeling good because of what you accomplish is a far more satisfying feeling and should never be mistaken for the pot high.

Since quitting pot I have found that I still have the same urges I had when I was smoking. I can still procrastinate with the best of them and I still get the munchies, the only difference is, I have no one to blame but myself.

As soon as the bust happened, I automatically reverted to my early religious training and was told by the Spirit that all this was happening for a reason. I was going to jail, and I was going to meet people in jail who would help me with my mission, whatever that mission was. I was told that the reason I had such good luck with the beginning of my career was because I was supposed to be helping others. The moment I started to think only of my own comforts was the moment things began to go wrong. This is the natural law of cause and effect. As long as my focus was on entertaining audiences, then the muse would be there for me. But as soon as the ego became involved, then the performance suffered because it was no longer muse driven. In order to be totally successful you must first be able to release the ego.

The one major problem facing the world today and every day since the beginning of this human experience is the false sense of self, which is called the ego. This puffed-up, pride-driven, false sense of self is the reason that the world is in the state that it's in today.

The ego is the personality we create in order to protect ourselves from other egos. In other words, it is our front. It is the person who we think we have to pretend to be in order to impress or intimidate other people. The real you has no need to impress or fear others because you are too busy serving others. This is our real mission in life: serving others, helping our fellow man. The ego prevents us from fulfilling our mission by demanding recognition or payment for its service.

I know the reason Cheech and I broke up was because of our egos. Once we obtained a measure of success, our egos slid in and said, "Thanks, but I'll take it from here." And maybe my ego was bigger than his, which when you think of it, is a great example of ego. Mine was bigger than his! There you go, the ego strikes again. The simple truth is, the only way any of us achieves anything worthwhile is through knowing God.

My last night of freedom was spent with my families, my children from both of my marriages. We all had dinner at On Sushi on Santa Monica Blvd. It was a very strained and sad affair. I could feel the anger coming from my oldest daughters, Rae Dawn and Robbi. Their mother, Maxine, my first wife, had called earlier to wish me luck and she told me to be strong. She felt bad for me, but she knew that I would survive this ordeal with no problems.

I received another phone call that last night from Pat Morita, the great Korean actor best remembered as Mr. Miyagi from *The Karate Kid*. Pat's soothing voice, filled with encouragement and love, stayed with me throughout my entire incarceration. He told me everything I needed to hear. He reminded me that I was going in because of the current administration's crackdown on weed culture and told me to remember that everyone respected me for what I was about to go through.

Shelby and I finally went to bed. Wrapped in high thread count comfort and the softness of my wife's smooth arms for the last time for another nine months, we slept, hugging each other all night.

October 8, 2003, at exactly six a.m., the phone rang. I picked it up on the first ring and heard the familiar voice of my answering service: "Good morning, this is your six a.m. wake-up call." I hung up the phone and then called back to cancel my service so Shelby wouldn't be woken up every morning at six for the next nine months or until her son helped her figure out how to make it stop.

"Who was that?" she asked as she blow-dried her hair.

"It was the wake-up service. I canceled it," I yelled over the hair dryer noise.

"Honey, cancel the wake-up service, okay?" she yelled back over the hair dryer.

I smiled. Small things like this, the mundane domestic moments couples have that normally slip by unnoticed, ranked among the things I was going to miss most in prison. The phone rang again. This time it was Steve, a writer from *Vanity Fair* who had arranged to pick me up in a limo, thinking it would be cool for America's number one stoner to arrive to jail in style. "Okay, the limo will be at your place in a half hour. How do you feel?"

I sat in silence for a moment and asked myself: How do I feel? Well, I wasn't tired, even though I hadn't slept all night, and I wasn't sad, even though my wife and I clung to each other the entire night.

"Tommy, are you there?" asked Steve. "Do you want me to bring you some coffee?"

"Coffee?" I answered. "No, we'll stop at Starbucks on the way."

I wandered into my office and checked the pile of stuff that would be sent to me after my incarceration. It was all there. My life's work, really, in a pile on my desk. My Gibson Jazz guitar, my Pignose amp, my computer for writing my book, and my Joel Goldsmith spiritual book *The Mystic I.* Everything that I would need for the nine months I would be spending in the Taft Correctional Institute in Taft, California.

I walked out onto the roof adjacent to my office and was greeted with a big, lazy yawn from my fourteen-year-old mongrel dog, Tempy. I named him Tempy because when I told Shelby that I was bringing home a puppy fourteen years ago, she said, "Well, that will be temporary." Tempy wandered slowly over to me and leaned against my leg. He was my best friend and a good audience. When I decided to go back into comedy, I used to practice my stand-up routines in front of Tempy. And he would sit there, looking at me with that perfect stunned look that so many of the audiences I have played before had.

"Tempy, listen to me. I am going away for a while, and I want you to look after the place for me while I am gone, okay?"

Tempy looked at me and yawned in my face again. He started to do his little tap dance with his long claws beating a rhythm on the hardwood floors. This was his way of saying, "Say, can you cut the bullshit? I'm hungry. Feed me."

Shelby appeared, looking like a fashion model on her way to an audition. "The limo's downstairs. Are you going to bring all your stuff with you now?" she asked, almost politely.

"No, just the bag of clothes," I answered as I stroked my hungry dog.

She looked at me and then disappeared into the house. We were trying our very best not to make a scene yet. After all, nine months isn't all that much time. I looked around the roof, at the empty pots in which I had grown some of the best medical marijuana in all of California. That was only a year ago. Man, how time flies.

The phone rang again. This time, Shelby answered and passed me the cordless. "Josh."

I could picture my friend Josh on the other end of the

line: nervous and hyper, like the neurotic New York film-maker he is. Josh was making a documentary on my experience with Operation Pipe Dreams, this cockamamy bullshit bust engineered by the Bush administration and carried out by his sheriff of Nottingham, John Ashcroft.

"Tommy, listen, Steve wants to ride with you guys alone, but I want to shoot this!" Josh says in his hyper Jewish voice as I watch Tempy pee against the empty planter, absentmindedly marking his spot for the umteenth time.

"Hey, man, did you hear what I said? Steve wants you all by himself, but I think it is important that we document all this. What do you think?"

"Well, I think you should document it too, but I don't want to piss Steve off. *Vanity Fair* is an important magazine," I told him.

"Yeah, but this documentary is important too, man! Okay, then just let me follow you and I'll shoot exteriors," Josh conceded.

"Okay. Exteriors, yeah . . . that'll be cool." The director in me couldn't help seeing everything from Josh's point of view. I imagined Josh shooting the exterior of the limo as it wound its way through the Grapevine and almost to Bakersfield.

"Honey, the limo is here!" Shelby repeated, yelling from downstairs. "Are you ready?"

I picked up my bag of clothes and followed Tempy down the stairs. Myra, our maid, stood and watched me with a sad look on her face, like she was about to cry. I went out the door and down the stairs making a mental note of this moment. It was a game that I played with myself all of my life. I would take note of this moment and imagine myself returning nine months later and remembering the feeling as I walked up the stairs.

I started this game when I was about seven years old in Calgary, Alberta, where I would lie in a field by my house, watching clouds race by and picturing myself remembering this exact moment, twenty years later. And now, almost sixty years later, with nine months in the clink ahead of me, I had vivid memories of all these moments to keep me company.

I opened the back door of the limo and watched my wife as she scurried across the backseat. I love seeing her doing simple things like getting into the car, showing me a flash of her gorgeous leg, or a brief look at her so very sexy bosom. I also love standing close behind her and becoming intoxicated with the smell of her shampoo and perfume, the scent of a fashion model. As I slid into the car and buckled my seat belt, a smiling Steve leaned over from the front seat. "Hey, man, how do you feel?"

"I feel like Starbucks coffee," I replied.

The limo pulled away and I caught a glimpse of our neighbor watching us leave. His advice, "Take the deal. Do your time, then appeal," ran through my head like a rap song. *Take the deal, do your time, and then appeal! Try to fight the Feds, you end up dead.* How true!

The limo wound its way down Capri toward Sunset. Houses flashed by. Goldie Hawn and Kurt Russell's house looked empty; they were living in Vancouver while their son played hockey. We passed Spielberg's house, surrounded by workmen's trucks as usual, and Nicole Kidman's house, a plain Cape Cod surrounded by trees with a guard outside in a Ford Bronco.

I tried to imagine the DEA driving past these homes the morning they busted me. They must have known all about my famous neighbors; they had my house under surveillance two weeks before the bust actually happened. I pictured them with their heads together, whispering to each other, describing what celebrity they saw in the star-studded neighborhood, chuckling about taking down America's favorite pothead. All that money wasted, when all they had to do was call me on the phone and tell me what I was doing wrong. Instead, millions upon millions of taxpayers' dollars went "up in smoke"—with most of the smoke being blown up George Bush's ass by John Ashcroft.

Shelby's cell phone rang. It was Josh. He was right behind us, trying to drive and shoot footage at the same time. As the limo pulled into Starbucks, Steve went in to get us coffee, while Shelby and I sat in the backseat.

"Damn! I just remembered something," I said, muttering to myself.

"What!" Shelby answered, sounding overly concerned.

"My extra underwear." A fan who had done some time in prison told me to wear two or three pairs of underwear in case they didn't issue me any.

"Okay, we'll just send Josh back for it," said Shelby, picking up her cell phone and dialing his number.

"Listen, Josh, you have to go back to the house and pick up some underwear for Tommy. Just ask the maid, she'll know where they are."

"Oh man! Don't make Josh do that," I protested.

Shelby held up her hand and continued to give Josh his orders. The lady was in charge and you don't argue with the boss.

Just then Steve appeared with the coffees. "Where's Josh going?" he asked as he entered the limo.

"To get Tommy some underwear," Shelby answered.

Steve smiled smugly at the news of Josh's dismissal. The twinkle in his eye gave away his satisfaction in having the media exclusive. We rode in silence, winding our way north on the 405, each of us taking sips of hot coffee, each lost in our thoughts.

I thought of Cheech. I had talked to him the day after I was sentenced and I could hear the anger and the sadness in his voice. He sounded like my son, totally outraged. "Those stupid fuckers. They just don't get it, do they, man?" Cheech knew, as I knew, that this was the government's payback for all the Cheech and Chong movies that ridiculed the hypocrisy and the racist, ignorant policies of the government's War on Drugs. The

DEA, Bush's private secret police, hated the way we portrayed them in our movies. Sergeant Stadanko from *Up in Smoke* represented a comic version of every DEA agent and narcotics officer in America. Unfortunately, the Feds took a fictional movie and prosecuted the actor and writer for exercising his freedom of expression. When I thought of it that way, I felt more like Nelson Mandela on his way to jail than a drug kingpin like George Jung from *Blow*.

The 405 was almost empty of traffic. The limo began to eat up the miles as we raced down the hill into the valley. *This is just like a Cheech and Chong movie,* I thought. Our car slowed to a sudden stop, avoiding a 1967 Impala lowrider that couldn't decide which lane it wanted to drive in, so it just rode in both lanes. The limo waited impatiently for the traffic on either lane to clear.

"Hey, I think we just caught up to Cheech," said Steve.

"I think you're right," I answered, glancing over at another Cheech, driving a late-model pickup truck. There were Cheeches all over the place. Of course there would be; this was Southern California. There are more Mexicans here than any other race because it was once a part of Mexico. This is a place where the minorities are the majority, a phrase I once heard up in San Francisco that didn't make any sense. If the minorities were the majority, they would no longer be minorities.

Driving in a sea of Cheeches, I thought again of the

call he gave me after the sentencing. He sounded like he was about to cry and his concern meant a lot to me. "Hang in there," Cheech told me. "It will be over before you know it and don't drop the soap." (If I had a nickel for every time somebody told me not to drop the soap, I could pay all my lawyer bills and still have money left over.)

Cheech and I had performed at quite a few prisons in the seventies. San Quentin was the most notorious of the level-four prisons that we entertained at in our "prison run." Located near San Francisco, just across the Golden Gate Bridge, San Quentin was and still is the real deal. This is where they put people to death in its infamous gas chamber. This is also the place where they put people in the hole for weeks, months, and probably years. The "hole" was really a hole. Solitary confinement in most prisons consists of a series of cells, complete with toilets and lights, isolated from the rest of the population. The hole in San Quentin, as described by Edward Bunker in his book *Education of a Felon: A Memoir*, was a bare cell, where the prisoners were thrown in naked to sit and rot for months on end in total darkness. Talk about cruel and unusual punishment! Anybody who did any more than a few days under these conditions, usually lost a bit, if not all, of their sanity.

I'll never forget the time Cheech and I performed at San Quentin. It was around 1976, and we were hired by

Ginger, a tall, gorgeous, redheaded stripper, and the girlfriend of a Hell's Angel who was doing major time in "Q." Ginger contacted our agent and told him that the "Woods" had requested Cheech and Chong to be part of the next show. Of course, we were thrilled to have the chance to play for such a captive audience.

We arrived at the prison with all our props and costumes, ready to entertain. The corrections officer who escorted us from the parking lot to the staging area was a well-liked screw and let the cons run the show. He was very friendly, but coplike in a quiet, threatening way.

We were searched, although not as thoroughly as I would have expected in a maximum-security joint like San Quentin. As we approached the stage, the CO casually informed us, "You do know that we have a no-hostage rule here inside, don't you?"

No-hostage? What the fuck was that? He went on to explain that if any of these prisoners with a tendency toward violence grabbed us and held us hostage, the prison would not allow the inmates to escape, even if it meant loss of life—namely, the hostage's life. I immediately thought, *Wow! This is a fine time to lay that one on us. But hey, we don't have anything to fear. If anyone can protect us, the Hell's Angels can.*

The show started as scheduled, with Ginger doing an almost nude, toned down version of her stage act. She would have shown all her goodies to the boys, but she had promised the warden that she would behave. As

Ginger danced, I had a chance to check out the audience. This was the scariest bunch of people I have ever seen in my life. Big, mean, long-haired, ugly, terrifying, tattooed bikers occupied the front three rows. They were staring intently at Ginger's womanly delights, trying desperately to memorize every freckle and every soft nook and cranny on her lush dancer's body.

The second wave of audience members were Mexican and Latino, and bringing up the back were the proud, defiant black brothers. The only thing they all had in common was the look of lust and longing as Ginger swayed and wiggled seductively. I glanced through a window out to the yard and saw a group of prisoners crammed into a chain-link pen. I was told later that this was the protective custody area, where they kept the snitches, child molesters, and other soft prisoners away from the general population. These poor souls were desperately trying to see around the corners and through the brick walls, trying to get a glimpse or at least a whiff of the near-naked woman.

I wandered backstage to prepare for our show, when a con appeared out of nowhere. "Hey, man, it's me. Remember me?"

I didn't remember the face, but I did remember the voice. This guy had been a popular disc jockey in parts of California. He had once ruled the air much like Rick Dees once did in Los Angeles. Apparently, this guy had killed his wife in a fit of drunken rage and was serving a few years in San Quentin. I called Cheech over.

"Hey, man, you remember this guy?"

Cheech looked for a long moment and then said, "No."

The guy looked disappointed, then Cheech laughed and said, "Of course, I remember. How you doing, man?"

He started to answer, but suddenly turned and disappeared as the CO approached us. "You boys ready to go on?" he asked, eyeing the DJ as he scurried away.

"Oh yeah, we've been ready," I answered.

"Well, hurry up because we have to end this show before four."

Ginger exited the stage to the loudest ovation, whistles, and screams I had ever heard.

"They really liked you," I said as Ginger ran up to us, wiping the sweat from her face with a towel.

"Go get 'em guys," she replied as she disappeared into her makeshift dressing room.

The convict emcee was onstage settling the crowd, which was still clapping, hollering, and whistling. "Are you ready for your next act?" he asked as the crowd roared. "I said, are you ready for your next act?" The loud roar became louder. "Then let's welcome Cheech and Chong!"

I think the most amazing thing about performing in a prison is the wide range of emotions the audience gives you. Here was a group of men locked up in cages with no contact with the outside world, watching and listening every second, every microsecond of every word that comes out of your mouth. These were men who spent their hours, days, and years reading and learning, devouring books like starving animals devouring meat. They would not look each other in the eye but they sure looked at us on stage.

They were so ready for Cheech and Chong. We brought their neighborhoods back into their lives through our skits. The first bit we did was the lowrider and the hippie hitchhiker. It was one of our most popular skits and would soon become the opening fifteen minutes of *Up in Smoke*.

Cheech walked onstage with the song "Lowrider," by War, playing in the background. Dressed in his traditional lowrider garb—a yellow wife beater, khaki pants with suspenders, and a green beanie on his head—Cheech pretended to polish an imaginary car until you could actually see the lowrider through the brilliance of his mime.

He then got into the car and adjusted the seat until he was in the perfect cruising position. After driving a few seconds, he pretended to notice what he thought was a woman on the side of the road hitchhiking. Cheech then pulled the car over, looked into the rearview mirror, and adjusted his beanie. He turned and yelled, "Hey, baby! You wanna ride? I'll give you a ride!" Then he said to himself, "I'll drive you right to paradise, baby."

At that point, I walked onstage with my shirt tied up in front, with socks stuffed inside to make it look like I had big breasts. I looked ridiculous with my headband, long hair, and beard, like some kind of hippie transvestite. The laughter of the crowd rang out as I got into the car.

Cheech looked at me with disgust. "Hey! You're not a chick. Hey, man, that's false advertising!"

"I know, man, but it was the only way I could get a ride. Nobody was stopping for me. I was freezing my balls off," I replied.

"I didn't think you had any. How far are you going, man?" With that, Cheech jammed on the accelerator, with sound effects of tires screeching and motor racing, and I'm thrown back into my seat as though I were being shot into outer space.

"First gear, rooooom, second gear, roooom. Hey." Cheech looked over at me and saw me clutching the armrest with my white knuckles. "Hey! You're not afraid of a little speed, are you, man?"

I immediately changed my demeanor from a frightened passenger to a concerned drug addict. "You got some speed, man?"

Cheech looked at me for a second. "No, I don't got no speed, man, but I'll tell you what I do got. I got a joint." Cheech started searching his pockets for his dope.

"Oh, here it is. No . . . that's my dick. Oh yeah, here we are," he said, handing me something. "Fire that sucker up, man."

I held up the imaginary joint and looked at it for a second, and then said, "I hope your dick is bigger than this. This looks like a toothpick, man. Hey, it *is* a toothpick."

Cheech snatched back the toothpick. "Oh, here it is, man."

I looked at the new joint. "Uh . . . give me back the toothpick, man."

"No, that's some really good stuff, man. I got it from my cousin Louie."

"Hey, you want to get high?" I asked as I reached into my pocket and produced a huge, bigger-than-life joint.

"Does Howdy Doody have wooden balls?" Cheech replied as I fired up the biggest joint in history.

"Hey, man! . . . Look! It's the Goodyear blimp," said Cheech, taking it from me.

"Hey, take it easy, man. You only need a little bit," I replied.

"What, is it going to blow me away? Hey, man, I've been smoking all my life. It's going to take more than this to get me high, man." Cheech took a little toke and tried to continue to talk. "Hey, man . . . this stuff is ah . . . ah . . . what was I saying?"

"You were saying 'ah,' man."

"Hey! What was in this stuff, man? I can't feel my face."

"Maui Wowie, but it gots some labrador in it, man," I explained.

"Labador? What's labador?" Cheech asked, confused.

"My dog ate my stash, man. I had to follow him around for three days before I got it back."

Cheech looked at me in shock. "This is dog shit?"

"It kinda grabs you by the poo poo, doesn't it?"

Cheech started freaking out. "I've never been this high before, man. Hey man, am I driving okay?"

"I think we're parked."

"Oh shit! We're being pulled over."

"How could we? We're already parked. . . . The cops are behind us, man. Here, take these pills," I said, giving Cheech a handful of pills. He looked at them. "Take 'em, man, I'm on probation. I can't get caught with drugs."

Cheech swallowed all the pills, at which point I told him, "Oh, don't take those."

"I already took them, man! What were they?"

I started laughing. "Man . . . you just took the most acid I've ever seen anyone ever take."

"Acid! I've never taken acid before, man."

"I hope you aren't busy for about a month. Hey! Be cool, the cop's at the window."

Cheech looked up at the cop and started laughing. "Keep on knocking, but you can't come in. . . . What? Roll down my what? Roll down my window? Okay. Coming down. What? Where's my license? Isn't it on the bumper? Oh . . . my driver's license. I got it right here. No . . . that's my dick."

In the meantime, I was eating the rest of the big joint, along with the rest of the drugs, when Cheech suddenly pulled his beanie over his eyes and began to yell, "I'm blind! That shit made me blind! What? Oh. I'm not blind. I'm sorry officer, what were you saying? Oh, what's his name . . ." Cheech turns to me and says, "The cops want to know your name."

At that point, I threw up on Cheech's lap. Cheech looked up at the cop and said, "His name's Ralph, man." The whole place erupted with laughter.

The sound of Steve's voice brought me back to the present. "Hey, we're making pretty good time," he said, turning to face me. He was ready to start the interview. *These New York writers,* I thought. *They do have timing.* I felt like I was on my way to a gig, which in a way, I was. I had nine months to finish writing a book, improve my jazz guitar knowledge, and work out.

"So what do you intend to do in jail?" Steve asked.

"Oh . . . I don't know," I replied. "I really have to see what they allow me to do."

"How do you feel right now?" he asked.

I looked out the window and noticed we were passing everybody. The limo was hauling ass, as if the driver was in a hurry to get rid of me. "How do I feel?" I replied. "I think I am still in denial. I don't believe this is really happening to me."

"It shouldn't be happening to you!" Shelby chimed in. "We had a license to sell those bongs! They had no right, arresting you. This whole thing is just total bull-shit! This is Bush's way of distracting the American people from his illegal Iraqi war. You're going to jail because of oil."

Steve looked at me as if to say, *I'm not going to interrupt her.* I gave him the look back, *Neither am I!* As she elaborated on her theory, I marveled at the mixture of love and lust I feel for this woman. I've been with her for more than thirty years. Thirty years and she is even more beautiful than ever. She looks so young and fresh-faced that she still gets carded at nightclubs.

The limo driver suddenly slowed down. "Ah, shit!" he said.

"What's the matter?" I asked.

"We gotta cop on our tail," Steve replied. "Okay, he's pulling us over."

The highway patrolman slowly exited the police car and walked over to the driver's side, stuck his head in the window, and said, "Can I see your driver's license and registration please?"

I thought, *Now, that's weird. He's on the wrong side of the car. He's on the traffic side. That is so dangerous! He must be an old-timer.*

As the limo driver searched for the requested items, Steve put on his New York charm and explained to the cop that the reason we were speeding was because we were taking Tommy Chong to jail and didn't want to be late. The name Tommy Chong seemed to ring a bell with the cop, who glanced briefly at Shelby and me as we huddled in the backseat. I tried to give my best going-to-jail look and silently prayed that Shelby wouldn't suddenly go off on the cop.

He disappeared for a few minutes and we waited, making bets on whether or not he was going to let us go. Everyone was positive he was going to let us go, and I think it was that positive attitude that caused the cop to return the license and registration and to tell the limo driver to hurry, without speeding.

We proceeded down the north side of the Grapevine, at what seemed to be a snail's pace. Josh called just as he was just getting on the 405 on Sunset, which put him a good half hour behind us. I could hear the frustration in his voice when I told him about the cop and how he shouldn't speed. *What a loyal friend,* I thought. I doubt I would have agreed to go pick up his underwear were the situation reversed.

We turned off the 5, onto 119. The sign said thirty miles to Taft; we were getting closer. I smiled as I thought of the way my name got us out of the ticket. Ironically, the same name was putting me in jail! Chong of Cheech and Chong. It was more of a title, a royal title. "Your majesty, it gives me great pleasure to present to you Chong, of Cheech and Chong."

The sign flashed by, eighteen miles to Taft. We were getting closer. Josh called. He was still on the 5, coming down the north side of the Grapevine. We were running out of time. I told Josh that we would wait for him in town. As we approached the dusty desert town of Taft, I looked at the little wooden cottages, the Burger King, trying to imagine why anyone would want to live here.

We pulled into the parking lot of a drive-through and got out of the car. Steve emerged from the passenger side and began snapping pictures with his little Kodak camera. Shelby sat in the car and waited while I changed from my street clothes into my prison sweat pants and white T-shirt.

"Oh, that T-shirt is too small," Shelby said, not looking at me. She had a habit of looking away when I wore something that offended her, and I did not look good in tight clothes. "You bought those clothes yourself, didn't you?"

"Ah, yeah," I replied, feeling like a four-year-old.

"Why didn't you take Paris with you?" She was really upset. As my fashion cop from day one, she hated me wearing clothes that she did not personally approve. In fact, the very first day I met her, she wouldn't look at me until I took off the dickey I was wearing. My band was called Little Daddy and the Bachelors, and it was part of our band outfit. I never had an opinion one way or the other on whether it looked good or not. I was a musician and used to wearing whatever I was told to wear. I just knew it felt good in the cold because it kept my neck warm.

She hated it. In fact, she hated our entire outfits. I thought she hated me. So when we dropped her off at the nightclub where she was to meet some other guys, I just figured I'd never see her again. Of course, she surprised me by giving me the sexiest "thank you for the ride" kiss I'd ever had. Her tongue in my mouth sent a shock from very the top of my head to the tips of my toes. My dick suddenly woke up and straightened out, instantly ready for action.

As she disappeared into the night, I limped back into the car, trying to find some room in my tight jeans for my still-hard dick. We drove on to our little nightclub, which unlike the one where we dropped her off, was not happening. Our club, the Elegant Parlor, was about to be closed down for good unless a miracle happened. The club, which was given to my brother and me by the owner of the building, had never caught on for a variety of reasons. Reason number one, no liquor license; two, no one knew we were open; three, we couldn't afford to advertise. I tried selling one-half interest in the club to the parking attendant across the street for a hundred dollars, but he turned me down because his empty parking lot told him the club was not doing well.

When we got to the Parlor, we set up our instruments and played a forty-five minute set for the waitress and the doorman, the only two other people in the place. We were good. We played all the hot R&B songs, from "Walking the Dog" to "My Girl."

Just as we were about to take a break, a group of people came down the stairs and stopped at the entrance where Stan was selling tickets. There was a brief discussion at the door. From the stage, I could just make out two underage girls accompanied by quite a few black servicemen from the States. So Shelby and her sister walked into the club and into my life. The guys were on leave and visiting Vancouver before shipping out for 'Nam. We played an extra set that night and were cooking; it was so cool playing for people who understood and appreciated our music.

I found out later that the other clubs in town wouldn't let Shelby and her sister in because they were underage and barefoot, so the girls stood outside and convinced everyone to come to our club, where she said she knew the owner. She changed my life that night. The club was packed every night from that night on for the next five years.

Of course, I have always thought that she was smitten by my charm and good looks, not to mention my dickey, and that she just had to come to my club to see me again. However, I found out later that she was enchanted by black guys, who were in short supply in Canada, and the only reason she showed up to the club that night was because she knew I would let her and her sister in. The fact that I was married didn't bother her, because she wasn't interested in me. And I knew I was safe from ever falling in love with her because I was in love with my wife.

Maxine was the perfect wife. She was tall, black, and very beautiful, and she gave me lots of space. She worked during the day and would come to the club on the weekends, usually Saturday, leaving me the week to be a single guy. One of the perks of being in a hot band was the fact that we attracted beautiful women. Maxine loved me when I played music and broke up with me the one year I didn't play.

There are women who love guys who play music. I think the reason women find band guys attractive, even when they aren't, is because they have to compete for their attention. Musicians already have loves in their lives, their music, and the stronger the music, the stronger the love. Women, especially beautiful women, love competition. They love knowing that they are so beautiful and sexy that they can make a man forget about his music, even just for a little while. Competition is sexy. What started out as a safe friendship between Shelby and me soon developed into a raging, passionate love affair that is still raging more than ever some three kids and thirty years later.

And now here we were, about to be separated for nine months.

As we approached the prison Josh called one more time, pleading and begging that we wait for him in front of the jail so he could at least document me entering my new home. But that was out of the question. I was told very emphatically that I was to be there before noon, and I sure did not want to start off on the wrong foot with the people who were going to rule my life for the next nine months.

The prison was just a few miles down the road from where I had changed clothes. Shelby was starting to tear up. Steve was snapping away with his little camera. The last few miles felt like a funeral procession, with me being the guest of honor in the casket.

CHAPTER EIGHT

Chûn / Difficulty at the Beginning
K'an / Chên

If we persevere, things will work out.

There it was, the federal prison, completely surrounded by miles and miles of chain-link fences topped by coils of razor wire. The reality of my absurd situation sank in as all the feelings of denial that this wasn't really happening to me left. Shelby clung to me tightly as the limo drove the last two hundred yards, slowly crawling over the speed bumps. Steve stared at the onerous sight of the prison. I could almost hear the words as he mentally wrote the piece for *Vanity Fair*. I suddenly felt like I was in a movie, shooting the parting scene, with "Via Con Dios" by Les Paul and Mary Ford softly playing in the background.

"Now the time has come to part, a time for weeping."

Tears flooded from Shelby's beautiful face. I had always loved the way she cried, because her mouth would part as if she were smiling. She clung to me and kept saying, "No! No! No!"

I whispered softly, "It's going to be all right. It's going to be all right." We held each other for what seemed to be a long time. I could feel the guard's impatience as he paced behind us. Shelby finally pulled away and turned and walked out the door with Steve. She never looked back and I knew why. The last night we just spent together, we talked about just driving up to Canada and losing ourselves in the wilds of BC, where we would live like Indians, far into the bush, where no white man would venture. She knew if she looked back, there was a chance that I would run, just hop into the limo and head to Canada.

My love for my wife was so strong that I could have gone to my death happy that day knowing that no matter what happened nothing could change the years of love we had together. I was in awe of the power of the love I felt that day. I could feel her love surge inside me, giving me strength to face my uncertain future behind bars.

The prison guard spoke, breaking the spell. "I'm sorry, Mr. Chong, but I have to handcuff you now. It's just a formality, so if you would put your hands behind you . . ." He slipped the cuffs on me and led me through the door and then removed them. This would be the only time I was handcuffed throughout this whole ordeal. I was then led into a holding cell and told to strip naked.

The prison guard, who was a fan, told me that I better get used to stripping naked to be searched because "this dance is done on a regular basis." I stripped off the gray sweat clothes that I had just put on and stood there naked.

"Okay, now pick up your ball sack! Now squat and cough!" (The squat and cough is done to dislodge any contraband one might have up his ass.) "Open your mouth and stick out your tongue. Lift your arms, now turn around. Run your fingers through your hair. Now get dressed and sit down. I'll be back to take you over to the camp in a while." And with that last bit of instruction the guard left, closing the door behind him.

I sat and looked around at the empty cell. It felt more like an office, because there weren't any bars—just thick glass. The glass windows enabled me to watch a cleaning crew of Hispanic inmates mop the halls and empty trash cans. None of them bothered to look at me directly, but I noticed a couple of guys sneaking looks at me as they cleaned. A woman guard appeared and asked me if I was hungry. She had a very stern, mean look on her face, but her eyes gave her softness away. I smiled at her, but when I refused the lunch offer, I saw the softness disappear immediately. Her eyes became cold as death as she spoke. "You're very fortunate that you are going to the camp. You know they usually keep the new ones here for a few weeks. I better check and see if you are supposed to stay here." With that bit of downer news, she left.

I felt panic come over me for a brief moment. I realized I was helpless. *I am totally at their mercy,* I thought. *They can do anything they want to me and I can't do a gawdamn thing about it!* Then the calmness descended over me once again and I felt at peace.

"I am with you even to the ends of time." Again the message "I am with you" came to me. I was sitting there contemplating who exactly this "I" was when the first guard appeared and said, "Okay, now let's get you over to camp."

As soon as we walked outside to a white Ford pickup, the guard's attitude changed and he became a fan, telling me of his favorite Cheech and Chong movie and how he and his buddies would skip school to see our movies. He also told me that the "camp" wasn't really a jail. It was a camp where all the inmates were nonviolent and allowed more freedom than the main prison that we were leaving.

We arrived at camp and I noticed a group of inmates hanging around the main door. Some were sweeping and raking the area, but it was obvious they were my unofficial greeters. The guard escorted me through the door, where I was met by a Hispanic inmate who greeted me with a smile and a hello.

"I'm Jimmy and I know who you are. Let's go and get your bed and clothes." Jimmy and I walked a few feet to the laundry room and were greeted by Lonnie, a con who had been down (incarcerated) for more than fifteen years.

Lonnie looked like a movie star; he was around forty with a strong weight trainer's body and a country music haircut. Lonnie reminded me of Irwin McCann, the old biker who gave me my first and only jailhouse tattoo on my upper right arm. Lonnie handed me my bed mattress, pillow, sheets, and blanket all stuffed in a laundry bag. He then handed me a bar of soap on a rope. There it was again, the old jailhouse joke—homo humor.

We both chuckled and Lonnie invited me to drop by anytime. This was an invitation I would receive throughout the camp from all the groups of inmates who more or less dominated the prison. I found that the camp was divided into groups usually along racial lines, but the "long timers," the guys with more than just a few years to go on their sentences, had their own unofficial club. I was in the "short timer" club, with only nine months ahead of me. But because of my celebrity status, I was welcome into almost all the groups.

After leaving Lonnie, Jimmy and I walked across the grassy lawn and into my dorm, where I was met by a female prison guard nicknamed "BB" (or Big Butt). She greeted me with a smile but with the attitude of disdain and superiority that all guards have toward prisoners. They must be taught at their "hate school" that the inmates are "less than human" and should never be trusted no matter how much you would like to. I found that a lot of the guards were farm boys and girls who had less than a high school education. The prison provided employment to this depressed Okie area.

I also learned that the prison was privately owned and operated by a foreign company and was supervised by the Federal Bureau of Prisons. The prisoners speculated on why the U.S. government would farm out its publicly funded but privately owned federal prison system. The popular opinion in the system was that being private made it more difficult for inmates to sue for better conditions. I personally have no idea why the prison system is owned and operated by a foreign company, but I am sure it has something to do with money.

In California, the prison guard union is the most powerful union in the state and has enormous clout through its political contributions. By contributing millions of taxpayer dollars, the union, in turn, allows the guards to dictate the prison rules. But all I knew was that I was in the system now and would remain in the joint for the next nine months.

CHAPTER NINE

Sung / Conflict
Ch'ien / K'an

Stop asking "Why?"

My first night down had to be the worst night of my life. The moment I crawled into the steel bunk I knew what I thought could never happen was happening. I was in a federal prison. And I was going to be there for a long time.

The noise of hundreds of men sleeping was unnerving, because it was amplified by the brick wall construction. The snoring and farting was so loud that I felt like I was in the middle of a jungle. I tried to block out the sounds by burying my head in my pillow, but that didn't work because the pillow was about two inches thick and made out of plastic.

I felt a wave of claustrophobia come over me. The bunk bed started to close in on me. I could hear the guards walking around, locking the doors. I was trapped inside like a caged animal. Sweat poured off me like I was in a sauna. Fear welled up inside of me. I felt like throwing up and I would have, except there was nothing in my stomach. I hadn't eaten for two days, but I didn't feel hunger; I felt fear. Then I felt anger.

I began to play the events of the past years over and over again in my head. I flashed back to the moments when the cosmos warned me about the oncoming tide of repression. The events of the terrorist attack on the World Trade Center on 9/11 played in my head like an action movie, and I remembered thinking the world will never be the same again. I knew, as I watched the passenger jet slam into the building, that the reaction would be one of revenge. And I knew that the innocent, hippie days of peace, love, and dope would be replaced by war, hate, and destruction. The more I thought about the effects of the attack, the calmer I became because I saw that my little setback was nothing compared to the horror of death and destruction that was coming.

I turned over and bumped against the cement wall. It felt cold and hard as I thought of my gorgeous wife, who up until this morning occupied the space where the cement wall now stood. I tried to remember the smell of her perfumed body, soft and warm, but the only smell was the one coming from the bathroom that was located right across from my bed. *How am I going to last nine months?* I asked myself this question for the first time. I really had been in denial right up until this moment. My body was going to jail but my mind kept looking at everything like it was a bad dream that I would eventually wake from, everything as it used to be. No such luck.

So what serious, horrendous crime had I committed to deserve nine months locked up like a dangerous animal? Did I kill somebody? Did I rape and torture some innocent civilians? Did I cheat old people out of their pensions and throw them out into the street? Did I invade a country? No, I did not. But apparently Chong Glass did send a box of bongs to a phony head shop set up by the DEA to catch people sending bongs through the U.S. Postal Service and making it a federal offense. That's right. The federal government put me in jail for selling a piece of glass that can be used to smoke pot. Were they serious? Apparently they were, because there I was in prison and there I'd stay. The noise in the dorm began to subside as I got more and more used to my steel cot. I fell asleep soon after and slept a dreamless sleep.

A loud announcement over the camp's PA system woke me with a jolt. "Garcia, Chang, and Rocco, report to the chow hall immediately." I could see that it was very early in the morning. The sun was just beginning to rise. I lay in bed for a moment, listening to the other inmates getting up and dressed for the day and I felt a sudden kinship with them. This was like being back in Canada at army cadet camp.

The bunk beds and the bathrooms were located in

the center of the buildings and the uniforms even looked armylike. I was expecting to wear an orange jumpsuit like they show on television, but instead Lonnie had issued me khaki shirts and khaki pants, army boots, boxer shorts, and white T-shirts.

I got up and made my way into the bathroom where the inmates were shaving, brushing their teeth, and showering. To my delight, both the toilets and shower stalls had doors! (The prison camp at Taft was designed for women, which accounted for the doors.) I grabbed my prison-issued towel and toilet articles, picked an empty shower stall, and turned on the water. The temperature was perfect and the water pressure indicated that the plumbing was well maintained.

The Taft camp had its own water tanks so some of the more obsessed nutcases would spend up to forty minutes or longer showering. I noticed a tall guy who looked like a cowboy, lathered with soap, as I dabbed a bit of shampoo and proceeded to wash my own thinning hair. I stayed in there for what seemed to me to be a long time. Yet, when I toweled myself dry, I noticed the cowboy was still lathering up and rinsing off, and he had been there before I even started.

I soon found out that the inmates spent a great deal of time grooming, just like monkeys at the zoo. These guys could put women to shame when it came to spending long hours in front of the mirror. At first, I wondered, *Why all the fuss? They're not going anywhere.* And then

I realized why personal hygiene was so important in prison. (And no, it has nothing to do with dropping the soap.) I learned that the only way to survive in jail is to retain your dignity. As long as you have your dignity, you have respect. And respect is what keeps you alive in the joint. If you lose your respect, you're done. The first person you have to get respect from is yourself. And being clean and taking care of your body is the first priority. Scrubbing the funk from yourself will earn you the respect of your cellies. (Never refer to anyone as a cellmate. Too gay.)

Some of the guys would do the exact same routine day after day without the slightest deviation. And each race had its own way of grooming as well. There were so many different kinds of people in the camp—black guys, white guys, brown guys, yellow guys, biker guys, gay guys, straight guys, crazy guys. Man! Every type on Earth was represented. Some of the black guys would cover their faces in some sort of white cream, giving a very tribal look to their ablutions. The bikers with their long ZZ Top beards were also a study. They would spend long hours in front of the mirrors trimming and fussing, getting the look just right.

Now, if you didn't stay clean you would be told first by your counselor, then the unit manager would issue you a warning, and if that failed, you would be shipped off to the "shoe," a cell block that houses "special inmates." You did not want to go to the shoe. In fact, you didn't want to break any of the rules in prison, because all jails are designed specially to handle rule breakers.

Some of the inmates had been transferred from other prisons, where they had served years and years without the kind of showers we had at Taft. To them a long, relaxing shower was heaven-sent. As I toweled dry, the cowboy in the next stall gave me some words of advice. "Hey, Chong, you better wear your shower slippers in here."

I looked at him and then looked down at my bare feet. "You ain't at home now, boy. You don't know what you might step on in here. Peoples been known to shit in these here showers!" I automatically started picking up my feet as he went on. "Yeah, I know, it's disgusting. But, hey, there are some disgusting people in here." The tall cowboy looked at me with a twinkle in his eye. "My name is Rock. And I know who you are."

As it turned out, Rock wasn't kidding around. Some weird fucker was shitting in the showers. Yeah, that's right—he would take a big dump right in the shower stall and then try to stuff it into the drain with his foot. The poor guys who had to clean up the showers were not happy with this new development in their already shitty job. In fact, they were very pissed off, as well they should have been.

No one could figure out who the culprit was, but the "shower shitter" kept it up for almost two months. Our counselor Ms. Strickland finally held a dorm meeting to discuss the problem. She began by telling everyone that "it wasn't cool to be dumping in the showers," which of course had us all laughing like six-year-olds. Well, everyone, that is, except Steve the Blind Gypsy, who quickly raised his hand to speak.

"Ms. Strickland, may I say something?"

"Go ahead, Steve."

"You all know I'm blind. Well, I can't see what I'm stepping in until it's too late. So I'm asking you not to shit in the first shower on the right. That is the one I use."

That had everyone roaring with laughter. Still, the shower shitter struck at least twenty times before the guys on bathroom detail set a trap to get the proof they needed. They devised a lookout system, watching the showers and running into the stall after someone had taken a shower to look for clues.

The surveillance finally paid off when one of the inmates followed a trail of shitty footprints to a cubical and caught the guy cold! He proclaimed his innocence but the clues gave his nasty ass away. The perp was a white-collar guy from Boston with a ton of college degrees and a home in a gated community in a very swanky area of LA. He was a very intelligent man who ran a huge operation on the outside, but he got into some government trouble over an ad his company ran that unwittingly violated a federal law, and he ended up with eight months in jail. He worked in the same crew as I did, so I got to know him pretty well, but I never would have suspected him. In fact, his nickname was "Mister Clean," because his job was cleaning the visiting room toilet.

The camp administrator had to put Mister Clean into protective custody. When word got out that he was the shower pooper, he got "rolled up" (all his bedding and personal effects) and taken to the shoe. One of the brothers paraded up and down the dorm outing the guy, shouting like a town crier, "Mister Clean is the shower shitter! Mister Clean is the shower shitter!"

Poor Mister Clean! He just sat on his cot with a dumb look on his face while the toilet crew who had been cleaning up his shits for two months plotted their revenge. And they weren't the only ones who had it in for him. Mister Clean had gotten himself into a few altercations with the brothers and he got a reputation for being a racist. So some thought the reason he did his business in the shower was because he had a thing about sitting on the same toilet as a black person. But if that were true, why didn't he just use the toilets in the visiting area—toilets that he cleaned? Whatever his true motivation, Mr. Clean's new nickname became Shower Shitter.

CHAPTER TEN

Pi / Holding Together (Union)
K'an / K'un

*We hold all things together by holding to what
is correct within ourselves. Our inner
attitude determines everything.*

When I returned to my cubicle to dress in my prison-issued clothes, I noticed that everyone had made their bed. I was about to make mine when a balding man in his late thirties with wire-rim glasses appeared and motioned for me to follow him. He reminded me a little of Dustin Hoffman's character in the movie *Papillon*. He walked me over to where a bulletin board with notices hung near the entrance of the dorm.

"This is where you look and see what work assignment you've been given." The bald man went on to explain the rules of the dorm. "Everyone has to work unless exempted by the doctor. Most new arrivals start in the kitchen, because that is the worst job here. You probably won't get that assignment because of who you are—"

I didn't know what to say, so I said nothing, and he continued. "Listen, I told Ms. Strickland we knew each other on the outside." He looked closely to see what my reaction was and when I showed no emotion one way or the other he continued, lowering his voice almost to a whisper, and said, "The guy I was sharing a cubicle with left this morning, and I don't want to share my space with someone I don't know. So go along with me on this and I'm sure Strickand will let you move in with me. I'm in forty-two, away from the bathrooms." With that, the bald man slid away from me and disappeared around the corner.

I immediately felt at home with this guy because he acted like I had met him at a party or some function because he knew some of the same music people I did. I learned months later that most of the inmates in camp were liars—professional liars. This is what they did for a living and this is why most of them were in camp doing time. And my first friend was no exception.

He was a good liar and he managed to get me moved into his cubicle by convincing the dorm supervisor that we knew each other from the "street." I noticed other inmates waiting for the right time to talk to me. Most were extremely respectful of my privacy and I was always accommodating as well. I knew from the prison shows we had done over the years that I would be among friends here. And I was—for the entire nine months! I have always been easy to approach because I know what it is like to be rejected and humiliated by someone whom you love and respect as a fan. I have always loved and respected my fans; I know if you like what I've done over the years, you are either a stoner or you know someone who is. All the inmates gave me space and avoided eye contact. I was in awe of how crowded the place was and yet everyone had privacy just by reading body language.

Jimmy, the guy who greeted me when I checked in, came up to me with a big friendly smile. "Hey, Chong, you better make your bed. If you get caught with an unmade bed, we get points deducted, and we need to win this week."

He went on to tell me how the counselors along with the camp administrator inspect the dorms for cleanliness and award a first, second, and third prize to the cleanliest group. The winning dorm gets the privilege of being first in line at the chow hall and they are also rewarded with a bag of popcorn and a can of soda on Saturday night. The prize sounded trivial at the time, but after a few months I was lined up like the rest for my pop and popcorn.

I was making my bed when Ms. Strickland came into the cube. I noticed right away that she was very attractive with short hair, a perky way of talking, and a very nice firm body. She reminded me of my daughter's skating teacher.

"Hi, Chong, I'm Ms. Strickland, your counselor, and I see you are making your bed. That's one rule we really enforce here. I would suggest you make it as soon as you wake up, because sometimes people forget and you don't want to break rules in here. Now, I understand you knew Mike on the outside, is that correct?"

I really didn't know how I should answer that question without lying, so I mumbled something about us having a mutual acquaintance at a party. Then I noticed she wasn't really listening to me. I came to learn that the guards and the counselors have heard every conceivable story there is to be heard and that most of them consider everything said to them by the inmates lies.

"Okay. You have to fill out a 'cop-out' request form and give it to the clerk. Make sure you put the number of the cubicle where you want to move." She studied her clipboard for a moment. "Okay, have you been to medical yet?"

"No, not yet," I answered.

"Well, they will be putting you on the list, probably tomorrow, so after you clear medical you will be assigned a job." Ms. Strickland continued talking but I tuned out what she was saying and studied her. She was a very attractive woman—why would she choose to work in a prison? And was she married? "So, you know what you have to do? . . . Chong?" she asked, breaking my study.

"Oh yeah, I got it! And thank you, Ms. Strickland."

She turned and walked briskly down the corridor to her office where a couple of inmates waited to talk to her. I wandered back to the bulletin board and studied it so I would know where to look for my assignments.

Around ten thirty a.m. the inmates began to gather in their cubes for the "prelunch count." I was not aware of what was going on and decided to take a stroll outside. I got about twenty feet from the door when a middle-aged Mexican came running after me.

"Hey, Chong, get inside, quick. You don't want to be caught outside during count!"

"Weren't we just counted?" I asked as he hustled me back inside.

"Yeah, but that was the morning count," he replied. "We got two more after this. And they are all standing counts, so don't let them catch you sitting. Believe me, you don't want to get caught sitting when you should be standing!"

The guard locked the door seconds after we came back inside. That was a close call—one of many I would experience during my nine-month stay. Control was the order of the day in prison. The prison staff was obsessed with the daunting task of controlling the prisoners to the point of insanity. They tried to control every movement of all the people in the prison.

Yet at the same time they were so detached from us that we could be invisible whenever we wanted. Like if you wanted to smuggle something into your locker, like food from the garden, all you had to do was act normal and walk right in with the bag in plain sight. The worst thing you could do was to try and sneak something in under your shirt, because that would attract attention.

I've heard that at many prisons, even though the guards know everyone has something they're not supposed to have, they would save their knowledge for a raid. The guards would collect overtime pay whenever the prison was "locked down," and the word was that "lockdown" would take place just before Christmas when the extra pay would come in handy.

Around eleven thirty a.m. the guards opened the doors and the inmates walked to the dining hall, where they lined up for food. I knew the grub would probably be pretty bad, but to my surprise, the food was quite tasty because of all the sugar and salt they put in it. The disgusting part of the prison dining experience was the plastic trays that the food was served on and the manner in which they would hurry everyone along, making the dining experience as uncomfortable as possible.

Dining in a relaxed fashion was a habit I had acquired over the years, and even though I was in prison, it was a habit I never really lost. Being rushed through a meal was never my idea of a good time, but I really had no choice other than to cook my own meals or have somebody else cook them for me, which, thank God, actually happened. Eric Larson, a golf caddie who had been taken down on a coke bust, was my saving angel in the food department. Eric, who was in the last two years of his sentence, approached me right away and invited me into his "car," or posse, which consisted of a couple of the more affluent, educated, and well-mannered inmates.

He did all the cooking and doled out huge portions to the hungry crew in his car. I could only eat a quarter of what he gave me at first. But toward the end I was scarfing it all down and looking for seconds! Friday was special because Eric would serve us ice cream and crumbled cookies for dessert. He would make an extra serving for the old black inmate who had been there for years—Pops, as he was known, drove the tractor and had to be in his eighties. Eric always looked out for Pops and other neglected souls, and he did it without fanfare. The only payment I had to make for this fantastic meal service was washing the dirty dishes and cooking containers. I eventually acquired some housecleaning habits that are still with me to this day.

Eric worked in the garden, so he had access to the freshest vegetables and greens in the camp. He, along with others, had built the garden area into a crop-producing farm that grew more produce than he could give away. Eric immediately talked the horticulture teacher, Mr. Ono, into letting me volunteer in the garden. A volunteer never got paid for his labors, however the sixty cents a day was not really missed by anyone. Oh yeah, that's what they paid the inmates—sixty cents a day!

The camp, with its incredibly diverse and interesting inmates, was located in the middle of a protected species area in the desert, meaning all the creatures there were protected by the state of California. I think they knew it too, because there were quite a few of them—creepy crawlies, giant scorpions, snakes of all descriptions, jack-rabbits, bunnies, and ground squirrels.

Things were starting to look up for me. I loved my garden assignment. I almost fucked it up, though, when I got so engrossed in my work I missed a count! I was busy trying to create a bonsai tree when an inmate came running over to me and told me I was being told to report to control immediately. I put down the plant and slowly sauntered over to the control area, where I was greeted by one pissed-off guard.

"Where the hell were you, Chong?" he barked at me like I was in the army.

"In the garden," I replied, sounding just like the stoner I used to play in the movies.

"What are you doing in the garden?" he asked, gritting his teeth. He reminded me of Sarge in *Gomer Pyle*.

"Uh, gardening," I replied.

"Were you assigned to the garden?" he asked.

"I'm a volunteer."

"What is your job?"

"I don't have a job. Well . . . except the garden."

He stared at me for a long time, giving me a chance to remember that I had been assigned a job sweeping a couple of sidewalks. It was the easiest job in the camp, reserved for old men and semiretards. The entire job took about five minutes if you hurried and about a half hour if you took your time.

"Oh yeah, my job is sweeping the sidewalks," I said finally.

"That's right, Chong. And you better get on your job."

"Can I work in the garden when I finish sweeping?" I asked, trying to sound as humble as I could. Of course, I was really thinking, *Please, massa, please let ole Chong work in da garden. Oh please, massa. I be good! I promise.*

I think he picked up on my thoughts, because he stared at me for a moment, then answered, "No . . . you stay on your sweeping job."

"Can I work in the garden when I finish sweeping?"

"No! Your job is sweeping. Now get doing your job!" With that, he turned and walked away.

I smiled at the way I was being "put in my place." The truth was everyone was bending over backward to cater to me, including some of the guards. The garden job was about the sweetest job you could have, because the garden was away from the dorms and there were no fences. If you faced away from the camp it didn't feel like you were in prison. And a garden is a beautiful place, anyway; it is Mother Nature at her best.

Everyone wanted to work in the garden, especially the long-timers. There was a waiting list a mile long, and for me to walk right into the best job in the camp was an insult to those waiting. But somehow, none of the inmates really seemed to mind in my case.

Mr. Ono, a Japanese American, liked me, and I think he liked the fact that a celebrity wanted to work in his gardens. I waited for a few weeks and then signed up to take a course from Mr. Ono. Ironically, it was a course on how to grow and maintain *grass.* I hadn't been in a school setting for about fifty years, so it was new and exciting sitting in class again. And it was fun. For the first time in my life I actually sat up and tried to listen and get good marks.

Mr. Ono eventually got me back on garden detail when the CO who banned me was shipped off to Iraq. He had relegated me to the task of sweeping up cigarette butts, which I actually quite enjoyed.

I swept beside a medical doctor, an acclaimed AIDS expert, who was so talented and bright that he looked at every task as an opportunity to learn—even if that learning opportunity was the best way to sweep up cigarette butts. It made no difference to him what job he was given, because he gave every job his all. That is the nature of a successful man.

The question I am asked more than any other is: "Mr. Chong, if you had your life to do over again, what is the one thing you would do differently?" To tell you the truth, I would not change a thing because: (a) it is impossible to do, and (b) what good would it do? You are who you are and I am who I am. Bottom line, in order to be happy, you must find a way to make someone else happy. This is the only way to truly be happy. Picking up garbage in prison made everyone happy. No one likes seeing garbage. Like the doctor, I found as much satisfaction in sweeping as I did in gardening.

Mr. Ono was very nice to me because he saw I recognized and respected his knowledge and his artistic soul. One day he had his workers dump a load of clay near my work area. He had dug the clay from his tree farm, and rather than discard it, he gave it to me. I loved working with clay. I was like a dog in a boneyard. I couldn't wait to get to my work place and create things. I made all kinds of dishes, cups, saki bottles, saki cups, and clay bongs that I would destroy immediately. I also spent hours carving spoons, chopsticks, and serving tongs from wood salvaged from the many pallets that were stacked for the Indian sweat lodge fires. The only problem was I had no way to fire them—that is, to bake them into pottery.

I went to Rick, a friend who worked in the library. He was one of the most intelligent men in the prison and, of course, knew everything about pottery. Turns out he had designed the pottery station over at the main prison and the one at the camp.

"What one at the camp?" I asked.

"The one where you guys play guitar. That was originally a potter studio," he replied.

"So why isn't it used for pottery?"

"We were waiting for a kiln," he explained. "But when

the kiln finally arrived, they changed their minds. It's sitting in the warehouse right now. It's been there two years."

"Why won't they set it up?" I asked.

"Don't know. This is the way things work in prison. They have the kiln going full blast over there. Not here though," Rick replied. "These guys like to break our hearts. If they can make our life more miserable by denying us anything, they will. That is just their nature."

"But making pottery is such a great way to spend time," I argued. "There must be someone we can talk to."

"Maybe you can talk to them. They might listen to you because of who you are," he said, then laughed, adding, "They would just send my ass back over to max if I were to ask."

Rick proceeded to explain to me how I could make a kiln from adobe. Adobe is the clay earth that is everywhere in the desert. The entire prison sat on adobe. The trick was making the kiln large enough and deep enough to be functional. The plan was so simple it brought tears to my eyes.

When I realized how much one could make from adobe, I began making adobe bricks. I built a rectangular wooden mold with handles on one end so I could turn the bricks over when they were baked, and then I mixed the mud and straw-grass mixture with water in a large tub. When it was the right consistency, I filled each clay mold and set them all out in the hot desert sun to bake.

After a full day in the sun the bricks were hard as . . . bricks. I then knocked them loose from the molds and stacked them around my work area. When I had as many as I needed for the kiln, I baked a couple of larger half-circles for the top of the oven and it was ready for the assemblage. I enlisted the help of my "dog," Steve, to build the kiln. ("Dog" is prison parlance for "best friend.")

I met Steve the second week I was in. However, we didn't become friends until around the second month. He was the first guy I met in prison who looked like a real convict. He had tattoos all over his body and was built like a professional football player, having spent most of his time in the clink pumping iron or whatever he could get his hands on. Steve was one scary-looking dude.

But when Steve first approached me and mentioned an obscure Cheech and Chong bit from one of our records and broke into a semitoothless grin, he became my biggest fan in the prison. We really connected one day when I was on the basketball court practicing my tango walk. It looks easy when it is done correctly, but to make it look easy you have to practice. So I practiced every day whenever I could. I knew I looked a bit weird to the other prisoners and guards, but hey, I'm so used to people looking at me that I feel weird if they don't. So there I was on the basketball court, walking up and down in the dance position, holding my arms as if I were dancing with a partner, when Steve started yelling at me.

"Hey, Chong, you don't have to dance alone. Hell, I'll dance with you!"

Steve repeated his invitation a couple of times, getting laughs from his group of biker friends. I didn't reply. Instead, I tango walked over to where they were standing, grabbed Steve as if he was my dance partner, and started dancing with him. He pulled back violently, causing the gang of bikers to laugh even harder.

"Get the hell away from me!" he roared, his face turning red from embarrassment.

"Hey, I thought you wanted to dance with me," I replied, still trying to embrace the huge bodybuilder.

I chuckle every time I think of Steve pulling away from my embrace. The big bad biker was homophobic. But he was cool and had a great sense of humor. Eventually, we started to seek each other out on the way to the chow hall and we would walk the track together in the evening. I found myself looking forward to hearing his stories of being locked up in various prisons and about all of his wife and girlfriend escapades. His first wife was named Ruth, so when they divorced he had his tat changed to "Ruthless."

Steve also taught me the different prison games, like dominos and a card game called casino. Man, I loved playing casino. We would play it while we waited for lunch and sometimes we played it through lunch. To make the game interesting, we gambled. Now, I really don't believe in gambling for money because I have come to the realization that to gamble for money is to mock God. And when you mock the Big Guy, you will lose everything. To be truly successful in life you must respect every penny in your pocket. You must never treat money as if it will always be there for you because it won't.

So when I started "gambling," the stakes were simply push-ups on demand. In other words, the loser would have to do as many push-ups as he lost in the game whenever the winner demanded, which made the game interesting, to say the least. We had more fun playing for push-ups than we ever could have had playing for money. Push-ups are good for you, so you win even though you lose.

Steve made a habit of beating me at casino every day as I slowly learned the game. Eventually, I started holding my own and we added the push-up penalty. That's when the game got very serious, as we both hunkered down watching each card being dealt. Steve didn't know that I had been practicing, playing hand after hand alone, so I was no longer the chump rookie that he was used to whipping. I had a system and I knew what I was doing. Plus, I can be incredibly lucky at times and this was one of those times. I beat Steve fair and square so he owed me twenty push-ups. He started doing them right away but stopped when I said, "Not now. On demand, remember?"

Steve gave me a dirty look but got up from the floor, and we walked out the door and over to the chow hall. I remember Steve telling me how inmates in the other jails would have the loser do the push-ups while waiting in line for the food so the other cons would see who lost the bet. I know Steve was hoping I had forgotten that little tidbit of information, but as soon as we got to the food counter I laid it on him.

"All right, give me five." I was smiling, but I was serious.

To his credit, Steve dropped to the floor and pumped out five push-ups as his buddies in line razzed him for losing to me.

"Who's your daddy?" asked a big hairy biker as Steve stood up.

"Fuck you," Steve replied while the entire lunch-room roared with laughter.

We sat down to eat our hurried lunch. Steve was quiet but had a little glint in his eye. He was showing me how a real convict keeps his word. He owed me fifteen more push-ups, and I strung them out for about a week, making him do them on command whenever he'd get smart with me. It made the time pass so quickly that I was beginning to see why people who had been to jail came back again and again. There was a sense of togetherness and friendship that could never exist out in the real world. Convicts become family to one another, families that some never had on the outside.

Steve and I played casino almost night and day for a couple of months. The last game that I won involved making the loser jump on a table and flap his arms like a bird while singing, "Quack, quack like a duck, I can't play casino worth a fuck!" I had lost about five games in a row, so Steve felt like he had a good chance of getting me back and added the duck song. At first I said no to the new bet, which caused Steve to invoke the age-old "come on, you pussy" comments. He didn't actually say "pussy," because those are fighting words in any prison. But I got away with saying it because of my celebrity status.

Anyway, Steve talked me into playing for quacks, and guess what—I won. Man, it was so sweet seeing a big, bad shot-caller squat on a table and quack like a duck! The first night we were walking the track, one of the bikers asked us how our casino game was going. I answered by telling Steve to "give me two!" He tried to punk out by saying he was going to do them all right then, but the rest of the gang told him, "On demand, Steve. You know the rules."

We stopped playing casino soon after that bet because I didn't want to push my luck. I knew that eventually my luck would change, and I didn't want to be the one squatting and quacking on demand. So we got into a game called boccie ball instead. The prison had two boccie courts that we would pass on our laps around the track.

"Steve, do you know how to play boccie ball?" I asked one night as we passed the court.

"Yeah, I do. Why?" he replied.

"Can you teach me?" I asked. I had seen the game played in the south of France and in Italy and had always wanted to learn how to play.

"Come on, let's play some boccie," he replied.

As we walked over to the court he briefly outlined the rules. It sounded very simple at the time, but as with most things, it wasn't as easy as it looked. This game became my obsession for the rest of my stay in camp. And I do mean obsession! The first time I played, I had beginners luck and I beat Steve. And did I ever rag on him for the rest of that night!

"Who's your daddy?" I asked him as we rounded the track.

The bikers ragged on Steve as well until we were weak in the knees from laughing. As usual, he took the ribbing like the man he is. But I noticed a look in his eye that I had not seen before. It was a little twinkle that told me this game has just begun.

I could not wait to get back out on the court and play the game again. I had gotten the fever! I had found a game that I was good at that did not require any physical muscle. It was the perfect game for me because my age kept me off the basketball court and the baseball diamond. I could no longer run and jump and catch the ball without making a fool of myself. I had become an old-man basketball player, with the geeky one hand set shot and no reactions.

I remember the day I quit playing basketball. This was back in the early eighties. Cheech and I used to play ball at the Hollywood YMCA with people like Les McCann, the great jazz player. In fact, it was Les who retired me with a hard pass that I caught with my face. I saw the ball coming, but I could not raise my hands in time to catch it. So that was that! And forget baseball or football. I was sixty-six years old and I wanted to become the world boccie ball champ. I had reached the age where lawn bowling was my future.

The second night on the boccie court did not go as planned. It went pretty badly, in fact. I did not score a single point—zero, nada! I walked off the court very quietly that night and the next night and the night after that and the night after that. It was almost a month before I even got on the scoreboard, and to make matters worse we were attracting a crowd. Everyone wanted to see the celebrity lose, and each time I lost, I became more and more withdrawn, until I was downright horrible to be with. Steve finally refused to play with me.

"I don't want to play with you, man! You get so down, it's no fun anymore," Steve finally told me.

That's when I realized how the game had gotten to me and how obsessed I had become with it. The good part was I learned humility. I finally learned to keep my big mouth shut. I had become a loud mouth pain in the ass because I felt it was my job to heckle everyone. I would heckle the baseball players, taking great delight if my words took them off their game, including my own friend Eric! And being a professional comic I knew what to say to get reactions. It really was my way of performing.

That all ended when I was humbled on the boccie court, let me tell you! The boccie ball will make you weep. I finally started watching how the pros did it. They practiced their throws for hours on end every day. Boccie ball taught me two valuable lessons: Practice makes perfect, and keep your mouth shut!

I began to practice every chance I got. I started skipping lunch so I could practice on an empty court. And it finally paid off. Steve and I played doubles, and although we won our share and lost our share, we wound up beating almost every team in camp. Some of the best players took exception and started practicing as well. Harry and Howard against Steve and me became the classic matchup. Steve and I could not lose—that is, until Harry, who had clearly been practicing, started making unbelievable shots, causing Howard to respond in the same fashion. They started winning so often that Steve and I started ducking them, because losing consistently is not fun, period.

CHAPTER ELEVEN

P'i / Standstill (Stagnation)
Ch'ien / K'un

▬▬▬▬▬
▬▬▬▬▬
▬▬▬▬▬
▬▬ ▬▬
▬▬ ▬▬
▬▬ ▬▬

No progress.

I spent the first few months in the joint sorting out who was real and who was fake. That's a tough job in prison because everyone in there is a good actor, especially the con men. The first guys I met—or rather the first to approach me—were first-class professional con men. These people were in jail for scamming people out of their money by being charming and conning people with get-rich-quick schemes. They would get together and compare stories of how they scammed huge sums of money from greedy rich folk. Greed is the con man's tool.

One gangster I knew from Vancouver once told me how he scammed his money from "marks" (or greedy rich guys). The scam went like this: He would borrow money from the mark with a promise of a 100 percent return on his money. In other words, he would borrow, say, five thousand and return ten thousand a day later. The mark would be happy to make the money and eventually would trust the con man because every time he lent him the money, he was always rewarded with that 100 percent bump.

Now comes the score. The con man would excitedly ask the guy for a hundred thousand for a sure thing and, of course, the guy would give it to him without question because he trusted the con artist. This time the sure thing would fail and the poor guy would be out the hundred thousand. The con man would "feel real bad about it" and promise to get the guy even someday. Now, if the guy hadn't gotten wise by that time, they would do him again and again until he either wised up or went broke.

I remember getting a phone call from my con man friend right after Cheech and I had done the first movie. He came at me with a $25,000 request that I knew I would probably get back with interest because he was setting me up! Had I given him the money I would have been hooked into his con. I told him I wasn't allowed to handle money and could not touch even a penny without a signature from my lawyer. I told him all kinds of excuses, but he knew I was wise to the game, so after trying to guilt me into giving him the money, he got pissed off and quit talking to me.

One thing that I learned immediately in the joint was to take my time, because that was one thing we jailbirds had lots of. Time is a factor that dominates everything in prison. Everyone is doing time—from the prisoners to the guards to the families at home—so everyone is acutely aware of time. And the fact that you are incarcerated gives time more importance than everything else. I used to think I would be able to do the things I had a hard time doing on the outside because I would have all the time in the world. I thought I would be writing this book, learning Spanish, studying my jazz guitar theory—oh, I had a list of things I was going to accomplish when I was in jail.

But guess what? It doesn't work that way. For one thing, you are never alone. Never. There is no escape from people in prison. You are constantly being watched, listened to, searched, harassed, and counted over and over again four times a day. It is impossible to get anything done in a meaningful fashion in the joint; at least, it was for me.

The only time I hurried at anything in jail was when I ran the track and I only did that for a few days. I had intended to work up to doing at least five miles nonstop, but my bout with gout put an end to that plan. Instead I just walked five to ten miles each day. Gout is an affliction caused by excessive protein in the body that attacks the big toe, causing swelling and extreme pain unless treated. I had the gout before so I wasn't surprised, and the many doctors in the camp serving time for various Medicare fraud charges came to my aid immediately.

They told me to eliminate beans from my diet because of the excessive protein they contain and they told me what to ask for when I reported to "sick call."

I limped over to the medical office as soon as I could get my tired ass up. Thank God the head nurse was a fan, because the standard procedure was to wake up at five a.m. and wait until noon in line with a mess of other seriously ill prisoners. She tried to shoo me away at first, but when she realized who I was, she immediately changed her attitude and gave me the pills without the usual bullshit.

The pills she gave me relieved the gout almost immediately and the side effects of the pills got me quite stoned as well. I was never comfortable with a pill high, so I donated the rest of them to a friend who was suffering from a variety of ailments. In addition to cutting out beans, I realized I had to change my diet.

This prison food was killing me, so I started to fast one day a week. The upside of the fast was that it sped up the time. I would fast every Monday, and I swear I would turn around and it would be Monday again. Fasting also gave me something to control in prison because I didn't have to eat if I chose not to, and not eating for twenty-four hours gave me total control. The first thing I realized on my fasts was how much time was devoted to eating. I calculated that we spent at least eight hours a day getting ready to eat, eating, and recovering from eating. The time I saved enabled me to put in time practicing boccie ball and sleeping. I napped every afternoon from two until four.

Fasting one day a week allowed me to partake in Eric's ice cream sundae Sundays. Eric had a friend in the commissary who would make sure we had our ice cream every Sunday. Eric would purchase a bag of cookies and crumble them into the ice cream, making the most delicious treat and giving me more reasons to fast on Monday. I would then slowly eat my way back to normal portions, so by the time I was eating like a pig, it would be time to do the fast.

I eventually got Steve into fasting, which made it into a contest. He was a riot because he loved to eat and it showed. Actually, almost every prisoner had a huge potbelly from the jail food. And these guys would walk miles around the track and still retain the gut. Steve did it a few times with me but he suffered as one might imagine. His cellie, Marvin, would tease him by eating with relish in front of him. And Steve would turn into a big hungry bear, mean and scary and ready to bite your head off for sport.

I challenged Steve to be a man and to quit whining like a sissy, which in retrospect probably wasn't the smartest thing to do lest he snapped and went on a rampage. But Steve can take a challenge, and to his credit he did lose his gut and started looking like the badass character actor he was thinking of becoming. I started telling Steve about the joys of acting, and he listened and started watching television and studying the actors instead of just watching the shows.

Steve is a product of the penal system in this country, but with luck and the grace of God he might break out of the cycle and become an actor. He certainly has the talent and the life experiences, but the question is, does he have the will? You have to want to leave the "life" so badly, you will do whatever it takes. And making it in the acting world takes total dedication, talent, and faith. And you can never ever be a criminal again no matter how hard life becomes, because being honest itself is a test.

Life is like playing golf. It is only worthwhile if you are completely honest. If you cheat on your score or on ball placement, you might as well just keep the clubs in the car and go for a walk on the fairways. The same goes for life. If you have to lie and cheat to pass life's tests, you have failed, because life itself is one big test. When I met people in jail, I would try to believe each and every one of them. But some would just automatically lie about the dumbest thing and I would add them to the liar's list I kept in my head. And let me tell you, it was quite a long list. But Steve was the exception because he was always honest with me.

I remember giving Steve his first I Ching reading. He was pretty freaked out by how personal the book's message was. That's the I Ching—it never fails to blow people's minds. Every time I give someone a reading, I come away with something as well. The first day I received the book in the mail I was doing a reading for myself when an inmate asked me what kind of game I was playing. Rather than explain the whole system to him, I offered to give him a reading instead. So I had Mike throw the coins five times, I found his hexagrams, and gave him the book so he could read the passage alone.

I was curious to see what he threw, so I remembered the number in order to read it later. Mike read the words slowly and carefully, and then, without a word, he handed me the book and walked to his cubicle, where he sat on his top bunk and stared out into space. I took the book back to my cube and opened to Mike's reading: "You have suffered a great loss. Close members of your family have been involved in a terrible accident."

The reading went on to describe the tragic accident almost to the detail. I asked Eric about it and it turns out that Mike's wife and child were killed in a car accident. Now, how did the book know that? A book, mind you, that was written five thousand years ago. Interestingly, the I Ching was written by a Chinese sage by the name of King Wen while he was in jail!

The version I use is the one called *A Guide to the I Ching* by Carol K. Anthony, who spent years translating the ancient text into modern everyday language. I can't begin to tell you how much this book has improved my life. Please do yourself a favor and get a copy. You will discover, as I did, that we are all creatures of habit. We go through life on automatic, which is fine—it's natural. But it is so much nicer knowing exactly what we are doing.

The I Ching makes us aware of the path we are taking without judgment. When I did the I Ching for the first time in jail, it told me, and I quote, "You are in jail for a reason so lose the 'injustice of it all' attitude." When I read that I was stunned! How the hell did it know I was in jail? And how did it know I was focused on "the injustice" that was dealt to me? The first thing I did after that bit of enlightenment was lose the attitude and start collecting the stories that are in this book.

I guess one of my favorite stories was about Lester, one of the oldest inmates in the camp. Lester was a legend. He was in his seventies and was a career criminal who had been in and out of the system most of his life. Lester reminded me of the old Jewish comics who used to hang out at Schwab's Drugstore in Hollywood. These guys would meet every day over coffee and exchange stories and jokes. Lester would have fit in well with them. He would have made a great comic had he taken the comedy road instead of choosing a life of crime.

The camp counselors deferred to his age and gave him a cubicle all by himself with a view of the desert. Lester's cubicle was probably the best in the camp, but his age wasn't the only reason he lived alone. He was pretty off-putting in many ways and most inmates didn't want to be near him let alone live with him. I personally enjoyed his visits.

Lester suffered from more than a few illnesses brought on by old age and reckless living. He had undergone surgery about a month before I arrived and was still recovering. He walked around in a hospital gown, untied at the back leaving his cheese hanging in the wind. He was also hooked up to a bag, which he toted around with him like a purse. A few days after his surgery, Lester actually joined the chow hall line holding his "piss bag" in one hand and with his ass exposed. Like I said, he could be disgusting, but he was such an interesting guy, so full of great stories.

Lester no longer gave a shit about anything. He once ate another inmate's microwave pizza when the guy stepped away to let it cool. He came back to find it missing and asked Lester if he knew what happened to it.

"Yeah, I know what happened to your pizza."

The inmate pressed him for details and Lester calmly looked him in the eye and told him, " I ate your goddamn pizza."

The inmate looked at the old man and asked him, "Why did you eat my pizza?"

"Because I felt like pizza, you dumb sonofabitch!"

"But it wasn't your pizza to eat!" he replied.

"Yeah?" Lester shot back. "Well, I ate it, so I guess it was mine to eat."

Lester stood his ground and probably would have fought if the guy had gotten violent. Instead, the pizza-less guy just made another pizza, only this time he never let it out of his sight.

Lester spent a lot of his time sleeping because of his ailments, but he always found time to visit me. I would come back to my bunk after a few hours in the garden and Lester would be sitting there waiting. He really was a poster boy for the life of crime, having been in and out of jail all his life. And now he was in the final chapter. It was sad to see how cold and unfeeling his final days were going to be.

The last time I saw him he was sitting on his bunk waiting to be transferred out of camp to a hospital where he would die. He did not want to leave, but he knew he had no choice. Still, he was as defiant and crusty as ever, cussing out everyone in sight. Jail robs people of their dignity. The uncaring and unfeeling nature of prison is the best reason to stay out of jail. The day after Lester left another inmate was in his cubicle, and his home of the past five years belonged to someone else in the blink of an eye. Dispensable.

CHAPTER TWELVE

Ku / Work On What Has Been Spoiled
Kên / Sun

*Correcting decadent habits of mind and
tolerating what is spoiled in others.*

The track, like the garden, gave us a feeling of freedom within the camp, especially because there wasn't
even a fence around it, just a chalk marking that
showed the out-of-bounds line. It was as if the prison
was encouraging people to run away. And people did
run away, sometimes five a week. No one really cared
to run after them because they were usually spotted in
the town or on the highways. Those who ran were
never allowed back to the camp and usually had two
years or more added to their sentences when they were
caught.

Fred, a con who had been at camp from the very
beginning, would entertain us with stories from the early
days. The camp, which was built as a women's prison,

sat vacant for five years until the BOP (Boobs who Oversee Prisons) decided to make it a minimum-security camp and shipped in a busload of qualified prisoners from other nearby California prisons. Problems arose right from the beginning because the guards transported their prisoners in a used school bus—apparently the federal boobs who were the masterminds didn't realize that it is against state law to transport prisoners in a school bus. They found this out when a highway patrolman stopped the bus and issued a ticket to the prison guard who was driving.

The prisoners on the bus were supposed to be the cream of the nonviolent crop. However, federal prison rules mandated they be shackled when transported anywhere. And shackled they were, except for a stocky Mexican prisoner who had wrists and ankles so huge the shackles did not fit around them. So the boob team simply secured the prisoner with rope; they hog-tied the guy and hooked him up to the rest of the chain gang with a simple knot.

The only problem was that the mayor of Taft, along with other upstanding members of the community, were waiting for the prisoners at the gate with a welcoming band and a host of dignitaries. They were expecting a busload of white-collar criminals, who were nonviolent and certainly not shackled. To make matters worse, the hog-tied Mexican had a bowel movement problem that he repeatedly reported to the bus driver, apparently to no avail, which forced him to solve the problem on his own midway to the camp.

Needless to say, the stench was quite overwhelming, so when the bus arrived and was greeted by the band and the mayor and the dignitaries, the effect was quite profound. The shackled prisoners, in a hurry to leave the foul-smelling bus, flew down the stairs, cussing and swearing at the guard who had refused to stop and at the mud butt who tried to hold it but failed. The band played on cue, which only added to the noise and confusion and gave the Mexican his own personal welcoming reception as he made his way solo off the bus, soiled and humiliated. The ribbon cutting ceremony was hastily performed as the prisoners were unshackled and led into the camp.

The camp was grossly understaffed and under-stocked, so the prisoners were left to pick their own beds and dormitories. Fred, who still resides in his hand-picked bed with the view of the valley behind the camp, recounted how the prisoners had to fend for themselves for months following their transfer. The chow hall had to be put in operating order and supplies had to be brought in to feed the unexpected number of prisoners who now called the camp their home.

During the first year of operation, visitor access was unlimited—anyone could wander anywhere they wanted. Various barbecue stands were set up around the camp, where the prisoners used to cook their meals. They had also devised a system that allowed them to slip out to the nearby motels for visits with girlfriends. Other prisoners would cover the count by slipping over the cubicles to create the illusion that everyone was present and accounted for. This practice ended when the prison installed the new count system that is used today. The camp was a real *Hogan's Heroes* kind of place for the first few years of its existence. It was an experiment that ended when the first prisoner escaped.

According to Fred and folklore, the first guy to leave the unfenced camp was a retarded black kid who could not understand why he couldn't go home with his grandma and his grandpa when they left after a visit. The kid's loneliness got the best of him, so one night he walked toward the lights of Bakersfield shining in the distance, lured like a moth to a flame. He had to swim across the California viaduct and was walking down the highway when a police car picked him up and asked him where he was headed.

Seeing how the kid was the first prisoner to escape, the cops had no reason to doubt his story that he was "trying to get to town." When the cops heard that, they kindly informed the kid he was headed in the wrong direction and offered to give him a ride to the town of Taft. Once in the car, the wet retarded kid told the cops he was really headed for Los Angeles to his grandma's house, and they immediately drove the boy to the bus station, where he called his grandma and she told the bus company she would pay for the kid's fare to Los Angeles.

As the story goes, the bus company was satisfied with the promise and the kid was on the next bus to LA. In the meantime, the kid's escape was discovered by the prison guards, who informed the local police, who in turn realized who the kid was and called ahead to the Grapevine bus station, where the kid was taken off the bus and returned to the camp.

The next prisoner to escape was even more bizarre because he only had one leg! He discovered that he could hop faster on one leg, so the authorities found the prosthetic one abandoned on the escape route. The APB on that one apparently made the cop's APB Hall of Fame: "Be on the look out for a one-legged escapee who goes by the name of Hoppy. He may be armed but only has one leg. Apparently, he can hop very fast, so approach with caution."

Now visitation is handled much differently. There's a small visiting room next to the control room with an outside smoking area. When the room is full, the guards stop letting people in, like cocky bouncers behind a velvet rope. This usually happens on holidays and some visitors have to travel sometimes hundreds of miles only to be turned away.

The guards would also turn people away if they didn't like their attitude. The inmates called these guys "haters" because the prison would send the guards to "hate school." They had to become dehumanized in order to cope with prison life. Most of the COs in camp were very nice. However, there is an exception to every rule. There was one guard with some sort of complex, who was mean to visitors just for the sake of being mean. He never gave me any grief, but he did hit on my wife in a sexual manner every chance he got. I found out from other inmates that he did the same to their wives and girlfriends as well. He would make them change their outfits if he felt they were too sexy or the wrong color. That's right, the wrong color!

Apparently, some inmate escaped by changing into women's clothes that were smuggled in by a visitor. He just walked out with the rest of the visitors at the end of the visit. They found a razor and the remains of his beard in the bathroom, along with his prison clothes. The weirdest thing about all this security is the camp does not have a fence and anyone can simply walk away. I would say about seven people left by the back "door" when I was there.

CHAPTER THIRTEEN

Kuan / Contemplation (View)

Sun / K'un

By one's thoughts one commands.

On my second day in camp, I walked the track with two guys who had been down for years. They were part of the elite group of prisoners, the ones who held the best jobs and were respected and feared by other prisoners and guards alike. One of them was "flipped out" from too much jail time and was now into a Catholic priest trip, where he gave every cent he could lay his hands on (which amounted to about fifteen dollars a month) to charities. David had once been a drug kingpin, handling millions of dollars at a time. Now he is the St. Francis of the compost heap, catching ground squirrels and keeping them as pets. The guards and camp officials decided long ago to leave this one-time-drug-dealer-turned-oddball alone.

The other guy I met that day, Howard, became a great friend and boccie ball opponent, as well as my personal typist. He typed most of this book for me. He is doing quite a bit of time for drug-related activities—charges that he denies, of course. Howard tested me the first few nights I was there to see if I had any criminal intent. But once he and the rest of the cons saw that I was not a criminal in any way whatsoever, they treated me with the most respect a man could ask for.

As one of the few Native Americans in camp, Howard, a tall, muscular Cheyenne Indian, used to run the "sweats" at the Native American sweat lodges, a recognized religious ritual in the prison system. The Indians actually had to take the BOP to court and demand their right to freedom of religion. The fight went on for years before the Indians finally prevailed.

And then there was David, our fearless chief and dauntless medicine man, a scary-looking convict with long hair and dark piercing eyes that looked right through you when he spoke. David had been down for many years with many more years to go. At one time, he rode motorcycles with the real baddest of the bad and had the scars to prove it. He wore the traditional headband around camp and always had the same intimidating expression on his face.

I remember when Howard took me for a tour of the Indian grounds. He told David he had invited me to join the sweat lodge and David just looked at me long and hard, not saying a word. I found out later that intimidation was the way of prisons. If you could be intimidated you could not be a part of the group, which in this case was the sweat lodge. It didn't help that on my first visit we were joined by a couple of the guards, who were told to keep an eye on the celebrity con. The arrival of the COs put a huge damper on the tour, so I just turned and found my way back to my dorm. I knew then I couldn't join the Indians without bringing all kinds of heat to the area, so I told Howard, "thanks, but maybe later," when he asked if I was interested.

To tell you the truth, I was so intimidated that day that I did not join the lodge for three months. In fact, I had to really get into the rhythm of the place before I knew where to go and what to do. But when I did finally join the lodge, I became hooked on the place.

The procedure was fairly simple. I had to attend the weekly meeting held every Wednesday at seven p.m. The meeting was held in the chapel and was more of a therapy session than a religious gathering. We would greet each other with the hand-to-the-forearm Indian handshake then take a seat. The chairs were arranged in a circle, making everyone equal. The sweat lodge leader would then call the meeting to order with a roll call and a brief mention of outstanding business. David would comment on events concerning the lodge, such as the wood supply and the condition of the grounds. He would then ask us how we were doing with the songs and if we had bothered to learn any of them. Each of us was expected to at least make an effort to learn the songs, which were sung in the language of the Lakota Sioux. I sincerely wanted to learn them, but we were not allowed to have tape recorders, so I tried to learn them as we sweat. But it was impossible because of the infinite structure of each song.

Located behind the camp buildings facing the empty desert, the Indian grounds were considered a sacred area, surrounded by large poplar trees that swayed in the desert breeze and provided shelter for the various species of birds and animals that lived there. If you faced the desert, you didn't feel like you were locked away in a prison. Instead, you felt like you were in a magical garden where the animals felt secure and safe enough to scurry around your feet while you walked.

The lodge attracted the good spirits and you could feel the vibe immediately. Someone had even strung up an old tennis net between two trees and made a great hammock. Over the years, the Indians had made outdoor furniture, giving the place a parklike atmosphere. David had spent years hauling fair-size rocks that he used to build a low fence around the camp. He had also carved walkways and installed a watering system so the area around the lodge was carpeted with a green lawn.

Every part of the Indian grounds was meticulously planned and maintained daily by David and the other members of the sweat lodge. They had constructed the lodge according to ancient Lakota Sioux design, using willows and covering it with canvas and plastic sheets that were neatly folded and stored when not in use. They had also constructed a large circular fire pit that could burn the broken flats and scrub brush and anything else that burned to heat the fifteen or so rocks used during the sweat. The fire pit also contained a small Indian style oven.

Howard proudly showed me around the grounds, pointing out the totem pole that he was in the middle of carving and the herb garden David had planted that was lush with exotic and natural herb plants, like yarrow, rosemary, lavender, and thistle, which he harvested for the seeds. Eaten raw, the seeds provided a supplement that strengthened the liver. We would crunch on them as we worked on the gardens and in my pottery area.

The trick to good pottery is maintaining a hot fire for at least twelve hours. My first attempt at firing my pottery ended up destroying our little handmade kiln. But our oven didn't quite get the pottery hot enough. So when I rebuilt it I made the oven bigger and longer so I could get a healthy fire going. I hunted around for wood and, thanks to Eric, I discovered a stash of oil soaked railroad ties. Talk about hot!

That weekend I finished making my clay plates and sake bottles and cups and stacked them in the oven. I started the fire early Saturday, and with Howard's help we kept it going until Sunday. The inmates that faced the Indian grounds were freaking out at the size and power of the fire, but no one informed the guards, so we were safe.

I had to wait until the middle of the day before I could get away to check the kiln, and when I got there, the fire had burned itself out. I dug through the ashes for my pottery. I had stacked the pieces on metal screens that I had recovered from the garbage, but when I dug through the ashes I found the metal had melted in the heat and all my pottery had fallen into the fire.

I was devastated until I found the pieces intact in the ashes. They were all whole, none had broken, and they were all fairly well cooked. I had fired up some pottery the way the folks did it before electricity. Rick told me the Japanese made their pottery exactly they way I made mine. The oil soaked railroad ties also gave the pottery a sort of glaze that made for an interesting finish. I was going to bring my pottery home when I got out, but I never made it back to the spot where I stashed them. They are probably still there somewhere.

Steve and I had to rebuild the kiln yet again because the fire destroyed part of it. But I was happy to have the chance to improve the design. This time I used cement blocks as the base and covered the entire oven with adobe mud. We had worked on it for a week straight when the assistant to the warden and various BOP visited the grounds to see what we were up to. They never talked to us directly; they just walked around checking out our little campground and the newly constructed oven, and it seems more than a few of the prison officials just came to see the celebrity prisoner. I would hear them ask their guide, "Which one is he?" then look over at me.

I found out later that the day after I left prison, the guards made the inmates destroy my kiln. Steve was among those ordered to destroy it, but he refused. This kind of behavior was so typical of the Feds—they waited until we had finished building it before tearing it down. They also tore down the hammock and they made David cut down a few trees. They also changed the sweat day from Saturday to Tuesday, and no one was allowed down to the grounds during the weekend. I started feeling responsible for the childish response of the prison officials, but then I realized this is how it is with the Republican power structure, pure chickenshit. And if you know what to do with pure chickenshit, you can have a hell of a garden.

CHAPTER FOURTEEN

Fu / Return (The Turning Point)
K'un / Chên

Retreat from the dark power of pride and desire.

Being locked up in prison really changed the way I looked at the world. Up until then I was living in a media-influenced dream state. In fact, 99 percent of the population in the United States (well, actually 89 percent because 10 percent are currently in jail) lives in this dream state, unaware of what is really going on in the world. It was once said, "Religion is the opiate of the people." Today, the same could be said of television and newspapers. And the truth is, you don't wake from this dream until you die or go to jail, where you are confronted daily with the real truths, which is that we are all prisoners of the media.

Big business now rules this country. The conglomerates control the drug trade—and I'm not talking heroin or coke or pot; I'm talking about the prescription, doctor-approved, legal drugs that have become a multizillion-dollar industry, and useless and dangerous over-the-counter, symptoms-hiding, addictive narcotics that have hooked millions of Americans into spending billions of dollars on their habits daily. These conglomerates are the bosses of the Republicans who now rule this country. They are the real drug lords who make obscene profits off of the lives of millions of Americans.

These drug lords own the media, the television networks, and the newspapers through their huge advertising accounts. They own radio stations despite the antitrust laws, because these guys are so wealthy they each have their own personal lawmakers that have the power to change whatever regulation is in their way in the name of profit.

I received an education while in prison and for this I will forever be grateful to the Republicans. Without their help in conjuring up a criminal offense to put me behind bars, in order to "make an example of me," I would have had my head stuck up my ass for God knows how long. I would have gone about my business, ignorant and not caring, because I would not have paid any attention to this. I would have been sitting in my music room, puffing on my bong and writing doper songs for my show. Jail opened my eyes, and now I won't be able to close them until I have educated as many people as I can.

I learned more about reality and religion in the nine months I spent in the system than I will be able to share in this lifetime. The fact that corporate America rules this country was the first realization I had in the joint. And notice I said "rules," not "leads." There is a big difference here. A leader walks ahead and makes sure the way is safe and secure for his followers. Jesus was a leader and a teacher, as were Moses and Muhammad. These men were leaders, whereas Herod was a ruler. See the difference?

Right now all of us are controlled and ruled by the corrupt Republicans. We are being told what to buy, where to work, what to listen to, whom to elect, whom to hate, and on and on ad infinitum. George Bush does not rule us. The Republican Party uses George as their spokesman, their puppet, the conservative voice to reach the common man in America. George is your typical Republican in every sense of the word. He is very simple minded and corrupted by greed.

The image that will forever be embedded in the minds of millions of Americans is the one of George moments after the World Trade Center disaster, when he was in a second-grade classroom reading to the children. The cameras were recording this tender moment when an aide entered the frame with news of the attack on America. George sat there with the weirdest look on his face for what seemed to be an eternity, frozen with indecision before leaving that classroom.

When you think of the failure of America's spy agencies in this affair, you begin to wonder: Are they really that stupid or are they really that clever? Either way, the attack did take place, and it gave George and the boys in power an opportunity to further their agenda, and now America is at war in two countries at a cost of trillions of dollars. And as long as George and the boys are in power, these wars could go on forever.

So what is the answer to all this?

I don't know. When you think of how many wars have been fought in the past thousand or so years, with each being bigger than the last, one can surmise that war is inevitable. When you read the Bible you realize that war was a very popular pastime in biblical times. And God was supposed to be involved in smiting the wicked and rewarding the good. We can only hope that "what goes around comes around" and the Republicans lose big time in the next five elections.

CHAPTER FIFTEEN

Ta Ch'u / The Taming Power of the Great
Kên / Ch'ien

Dealing with crescendo-of-awfulness situations.

For the duration of my first week in the joint, I would lie in bed each night, rehashing my life. I remember tripping back to when my mom died. It is kind of strange that when you get put in a situation that is beyond your control, your thoughts go to your mother. I guess it is because in most homes the mother is the one who picks you up when you fall and is the one person who will stand by you no matter what. I know she was always first in my mind whenever something big happened to me.

When my mom died in 1981 and passed into the next plane of existence, I was shocked—more than I could have possibly imagined. I was in Sardinia, off the coast of Italy, when I got the call from my brother. I had just talked to my mother a few days earlier. I called her to tell her of the trip I was planning for her and Pop. I had arranged to have both of them come to Paris, where I was about to start production on *The Corsican Brothers*. She sounded very upbeat, and although she was frail and weak from a recent bout with a cold, there was nothing in her voice that gave me any hint that she would die any time soon.

She had survived so many brushes with death that we all thought she was invincible. She had survived TB so serious that the doctors had removed her left lung. She had even been struck and run over by a car. But her greatest accomplishment was surviving fifty years of Alberta winters.

The last time we spoke, she did make me promise to take care of my brother and sister financially, and she told me how proud she was of my success. My mother had been my biggest cheerleader throughout my life and supported me no matter what direction I took. When I quit school, she was the first to say she understood and never once criticized me for my show-business dreams.

She used to wake up in the middle of the night to cook a meal for my father when he drove a truck at night, and that habit spilled over to us kids when we started working weird hours. My father always worked for a wage and barely made enough to feed us and pay the mortgage. I always had some kind of delivery job or a newspaper route, and my brother and I always worked the summer vacations when we didn't attend army cadet camp. Even the army cadet camp paid money for attending the six-week course. It wasn't a whole lot ($125), but it bought our school clothes.

Mom took in foster kids and boarders for her extra money, and she always thought of others before she thought of her own needs. She was a special lady with a special heart full of love for all who came within her sphere. I guess no one is ever really ready to experience the death of one's mother. I know I wasn't. I wandered down to the Sardinian beach after I got the call and cried like a baby. Mom was my biggest supporter all my life and now she was gone. I stayed on the beach crying until Shelby found me and held me. The sadness stayed with me and, to this day, I can still feel the pain I felt when she left.

But my sorrow was mild compared to my father's. Pop was devastated beyond belief. We arrived back in Canada to find the family gathered for the services. My brother arranged to have a bagpiper pipe Mom into the next world in keeping with her Scottish and Irish heritage. And I organized a church service at a quaint little church down the road from where she lived. Mom wasn't exactly a church person, but she made sure all us kids went to Sunday school and she called herself a Christian.

Pop really had no religion, so he went along with whatever Mom did, but he always retained the Chinese philosophy that was ingrained in him. He did not understand death though. Right after the services, Pop got in his car and disappeared for a couple of weeks. We found out later that he drove back to Calgary to where he and Mom lived most of their lives and went looking for her in all the places they'd been together. He could not understand why she wasn't there with him as she had always been.

The day of the funeral, the house was full of relatives. I found Stan and we both decided I should take Pop for a ride away from the crowd. When we got into the car, Pop grabbed my hand and held it like a lost little boy. I started telling him a bit of the Buddhist theory that the spirit of the deceased hangs around for a few days and even months before departing for good. I asked Pop if anything strange had happened after Mom died, and he told me about an event that made the hair on the back of my neck stand up.

He told me how Mom used to love to sit and watch birds feed in the tide pools in front of their house in Vancouver Island. One heron in particular caught her eye because it was so big. Right after Mom died, Pop was sitting on the deck overlooking the beach, thinking of her, when the big heron suddenly flew up to where Pop was sitting and perched on Mom's chair next to Pop! The bird had never done that before and it has never done that since. It sat next to Pop for a good half hour before it flew back to the tide pools.

"That was Mom's spirit inside that bird," I said softly. "That was her telling you that she will always be near you no matter where you go. People don't really leave when they die. We become what we always were—pure spirit. And as pure spirit, we can travel anywhere and be in anything or anyone we so desire."

I know my talk with my pop helped him understand, because he changed and after a time he became his old self again. At the time, we were filming the Cheech and Chong movies. He even appeared in *The Corsican Brothers* in a walk-on role as a cook. I don't know if his scene made the cut, but he was in the movie. I put all our families in that movie—Cheech's wife, Rikki, and their daughter, Carmen; my wife, Shelby, and our son, Paris; my daughter Robbi from my first marriage with her mother, Maxine; Rae Dawn, my oldest daughter, appeared in the beginning of the movie as a gypsy fortune-teller.

I had a great time on *The Corsican Brothers* as the writer and director. However, I paid a huge price for my indulgences. Cheech and Rikki were having their problems and split up right after we finished the movie. Sadly, the split included my partnership with Cheech, and *The Corsican Brothers* would be the last Cheech and Chong movie we would make together. It was as if Cheech divorced me along with Rikki. I kind of felt the cool breeze in our relationship during that time and, in fact, I wrote some of it into the movie. The magic bond that had survived seven albums and five movies was fading into the past, and Cheech no longer wanted to follow this "crazy Chinaman."

I remember doing a scene with Shelby with Cheech directing, and he saw I had already replaced him. Again, I felt the change in him. He saw how easily Shelby and I worked off of each other, and I think he knew who would be there beside me long after he had departed. And he was right. Shelby and I are truly partners in life, as well as onstage.

When I went on the road with my solo act, I missed having a partner and I especially missed being away from my love, even for a few days. So when I was offered a gig in Guam, I offered Shelby a job. She had been studying acting with different acting teachers in LA and had been going out on auditions. I came to realize she was serious about pursuing an acting career, so of course she accepted right away and we flew to Guam to begin a new era in our lives.

Shelby had been there in the beginning when Cheech and I formed our act, so she knew the routine of writing and performing. And with her acting chops it didn't take long before she was doing quality "time." I took a bit of flack from other comics for putting my wife into the act, but I knew what I was doing would eventually pay off. And I'll tell you it sure made the road a lot more attractive.

Performing has a magic that only performers can truly understand. There is no better way to live your life than giving to others. Making people laugh and feel good is what life is all about! A comedian wields more power than the most connected politician on Earth. We make people laugh—and people love to laugh; in fact, they need to laugh, because life cannot be enjoyed to the fullest without laughter.

My first week down was certainly devoid of laughter. I was held incommunicado because the money that was deposited in my name had to "clear accounting" before I could call home on the telephone. The prison issued us each a credit card with our picture on it, and we were allowed to spend two hundred dollars a month in the commissary. That's where we would shop for chicken in vacuum-sealed packages, fresh fruit, peanuts, chocolate bars, shaving gear, and other necessities. Once you reached your limit, you were not allowed to buy anything else until the next month. We were also allowed a hundred minutes of telephone time per month. Cell phones were not allowed. And if an inmate were to be found with one, he would end up in the seg unit doing months of solitary time. I never saw a cell phone the entire time I was there, and even if I did, I sure would not write about it!

Not being able to talk to my wife and family regularly was one of the toughest things I have ever gone through. This was the only time I felt totally helpless and angry in prison. Being locked up makes you bitter and angry with everyone, a feeling I had not felt for years. However, my attitude changed when I talked to cons who hadn't talked to or even seen their families for years. I was constantly getting reality checks from guys whose lives were a thousand times more fucked up than mine. The length of my sentence was a joke to the guys who had years and years to go before they went home. It didn't take me long to put everything into perspective. I started grooving on the feeling of excitement I felt when I was allowed to call home.

Paris had moved back home so he could attend Santa Monica College, and he stayed by the telephone waiting for me to call. When I heard his voice the feeling of love and joy was indescribable.

"Hello?" The line went dead for about ten seconds while the operator asked if he would accept a call from federal prison. "Dad? You okay? We have been trying to call you, but they said you had to be processed through the system. Where are you?" Paris sounded concerned.

"Hi, son. I'm in Taft. Is mom there?" I hadn't heard Shelby's voice in what seemed like ages.

"No, she's not home yet. You okay?"

"Yeah, I'm fine."

"What's it like there? They told mom she could call you, but she tried and they said you have to call her. How come you didn't call? She was really worried about you. You okay?" Paris was so worried about his dad and I know he was feeling guilty because I took the rap for the pipe company. But the truth was, I was destined to take this little trip. There are no accidents in this life. Everything happens for a reason.

When I finally talked to Shelby I felt like a love-struck teenager. I totally forgot that the prison's internal cops listened in on the inmates' conversations, so I told her about the nice prison guard who visited me and told me how he was a huge fan of Cheech and Chong. I went on about how cool everyone was to me and how I was the big celebrity. We burned up quite a bit of my phone time before I finally said good night and hung up.

I don't think I was back in my cubicle five minutes when I was summoned over the loud speaker to "report to control." The other inmates showed me the way and within minutes I was standing at control, waiting to be escorted into the camp supervisor's office. The gestapo-looking dudes who met me at the prison gates when I arrived escorted me into the office and told me to have a seat. I sat down and waited to be told why I was there.

The bigger dude started by asking, "Who was the CO who visited you last night?" He saw the surprised look on my face and reminded me that they listen in on telephone calls. I smiled and told them I didn't know who he was.

"Was he Hispanic?" he asked, looking intently into my eyes, searching for the tell.

"You know, I don't know," I said.

He smiled because he knew I wasn't about to give anyone up for any reason. "Well, just so you know, all the personnel here have been given orders to treat you like any other prisoner and not to ask you for autographs or pictures. You are under no obligation to give the personnel autographs, and we expect you to report any prison personnel who ignores these rules. Is that clear?"

"Yes, sir," I answered.

I was cracking up inside because of these stupid rules. It seemed to me the guards were treated harsher than the prisoners in some instances. The prisoners were free to ask me for anything, but the prison staff was not. It seemed my main task in prison was to pose for pictures with the population. But the guards were under strict orders not to be friendly. I was to be treated like every other inmate.

So I learned quickly not to joke with the guards, because the BOP's biggest worry is a compromised guard. Prison lore is rife with stories of guards who bring dope into the joint for the addicts. Guards don't mind prisoners getting high, especially addicts, because their lows can pose a bigger threat than their highs. A stoned-out prisoner will be passive and nonthreatening, whereas a junkie without his drugs can be dangerously unpredictable, especially in a prison environment. Much like the television show *Oz*. Hey, if I was a guard I would make sure all the dangerous guys were medicated!

CHAPTER SIXTEEN

Li / The Clinging, Fire
Li / Li

*Through detachment and acceptance we acquire
a moderate and just view of things.*

America does not have a clue what goes on in its
prisons. Talk about corruption! The federal prison
camp that I was in is a study in waste, both in money
and lives. What the public doesn't know is that hazard
duty pays the guards something like double overtime.
A hazard is classified as a prison riot breaking out
that puts the guards in danger, which makes sense.
However, the guards have a perverse incentive to
create the circumstance—in other words, pick on a
violent prisoner until he snaps. They'll talk about the
prisoner's wife or girlfriend, suggesting that she might
be fucking someone else. And in some cases, the
guards might start a rumor that affects the delicate
social balance in the joint or put a rival gang member

in with the wrong people and wait for the violence to begin.

When the shit hits the fan, the guards don their riot gear and start kicking ass, beating people until they get tired, then they lock everyone down. Getting double overtime when the prison is locked down is a joke because there is no threat! In fact, the guards now have less work to do then before and everyone gets paid for doing nothing.

Diesel therapy is another scam that the prison guards love because it also pays well. What they do is wake up the inmates, shackle them, put them on a bus, and then transport them all over the country for no reason other then to rack up miles so they can be paid double overtime. The prisoners suffer because they are shackled and stuffed into overcrowded vans and driven for as long as twelve hours without breaks. Prisoners have been known to soil themselves because they were refused bathroom stops. They are treated like animals— actually, in some cases, worse than animals. And no prisoner is exempt. Old, young, disabled, retarded, makes no difference to the overtimers. The U.S. prison system is an international disgrace.

You learn to appreciate life and freedom more once you've done time, but I can also understand why people return to jail. You need the conflict in order to enjoy freedom. You need the dark in order to appreciate the light. Nothing exists without conflict and contrast.

Opposites. Yin and yang. Good and bad. Up and down. Democrats and Republicans. One does not exist without the other. Understanding this principle will free you from feeling sorry for yourself, which is another huge waste of time.

Being an inmate is a totally controlled way to live without the hassle of supporting a family, or even yourself, for that matter. It is no wonder the return rate is so high. In effect, the prison system encourages convicts to return by not offering them incentives to stay out. After cutbacks, prisoners get a bus ticket and five dollars when they leave. You have to pity the ones who don't have family or friends to take them in.

I watched one guy who was about to be released go through what seemed to be prison-withdrawal pains. Tattoo Steve, an ex-biker in jail for some sort of drug-related crime, used to laugh a lot and seemed to enjoy the prison routine, especially the "egg race." The egg race happened on Saturday mornings, when the dining room would serve "eggs as you like them"—fried, sunny-side up, or over easy—and the cons would race to the mess hall to be first in line.

We were released to go to breakfast based upon how well we did during dorm inspection; the cleanest got to go first and the rest according to how they placed. The ones who didn't care usually lost, and the ones who did care really had a rivalry going. Tattoo Steve was in our dorm and on the cleaning crew, so our dorm won pretty regularly and Steve would speed walk to the dining area.

Tattoo Steve loved the egg-day race, but a few weeks before his release, Steve stopped racing on egg day. I remember the day he quit because the vibe in the dorm changed. I saw Tattoo Steve sitting alone on the grass by the storm drain. His body language told us all to stay away. I saw him late at night when I got up to pee. He would sit and stare out the window into the night, listening to his earphone radio. Then one day Tattoo Steve was gone. And eventually the other inmates quit racing for the eggs. It seemed somehow the race was not the same without Tattoo Steve. About a month after his release, we heard he died of a drug overdose. His image haunts me to this day.

Tattoo Steve was so full of life in jail, yet he couldn't handle the freedom outside. I know his story is far from unique. So many people become "institutionalized" and it almost seems silly to even release them. One thing prison gives the unfortunate ones in our society, besides education and free health care, is a number. When you become a prisoner you are issued a number and that number has to be accounted for 24/7. When the prisoner is released into the "free world," he loses that number and is suddenly faced with the cold fact that no one cares.

You get attention in prison, and so many people need that attention. Usually sick people require the most, but stealing is a sickness that needs to be treated along with gambling. There are so many people in jail because of the addiction to gambling that something needs to be done to address the problem. I feel that pot could help in getting people off their addictions.

Now, you might ask why would I say something like that. Well, look at what pot has to offer. It's physically a nonaddictive substance with the power to alter short-term memory! My own theory, totally untested but provocative, is that the reason activities like gambling and stealing are so addictive is a problem that lies within our bodies. When our body is threatened with harm or even death it floods our system with natural drugs that act as painkillers and give us incredible strength and clarity.

The natural substance called adrenaline is about the best high one could have without breaking the law. This is the drug that John Travolta injected into Uma Thurman in the movie *Pulp Fiction* when she accidentally snorted his heroin. The adrenaline shot actually brought her back to life. This is the same feeling you get when you stand unprotected on the edge of a tall building or even on the balcony of a high rise. It's a form of speed high that meth freaks and crackheads kill themselves trying to duplicate. And it is within us waiting for a life-threatening situation before it activates. This is the same drug that propels athletes to great heights. Adrenaline, the natural drug of champions!

And it stands to reason, pot does negate that high.

I've known pro athletes who smoke pot to come down from that adrenaline high they get after a game. I've heard of cops doing the same thing to come down from the highs and the stresses of the job. I once went on a police ride-along, where I rode with a cop for one night. It was the most exciting night of my life and the cop I rode with said it is like that and more every night. It took me a month before I started sleeping normally again and that was only after one night.

All the addictive pastimes like gambling, stealing, armed robbery, rape, and home invasion are directly or indirectly caused by the search for that special thrill that only the adrenaline rush can provide. And the one natural substance that has proved it can control and negate that rush is presently illegal. Not only is it illegal, but apparently no one is even testing this herb to see what effects it does have on people.

One thing for sure is that unlike legal drugs such as alcohol and cigarettes, people don't die from the effects of pot. This fact alone seems to me to be a logical reason for the government to find out why no one has died from pot. I know it is economics, but come on, folks, we all know that pot is America's number one cash crop. The only trouble is that jails in America come in a close second.

CHAPTER SEVENTEEN

Ch'ien / Modesty
K'un / Kên

*Go forward constantly, conscientiously,
despite mistakes.*

I hold the record of being the second highest receiver of mail in Taft history. The reigning champion is still Michael Milken, the junk-bond king. I did receive a ton of mail and it was quite a thrill having my name called so frequently. They finally just started handing me the mail without saying my name.

On average, I must have received at least five to ten pieces of mail a day for nine months. I even received a few lonely hearts letters, which I turned over to a couple of my fellow inmates to answer, and as far as I know, the young ladies and inmates still write to each other. I am embarrassed to say I owe so many people letters and I intend to write as soon as I quit procrastinating.

When I was close to being released from prison, Steve and I decided to use mail call to play an April Fools' Day prank on John, one of the local jailhouse "lawyers" who was always bending my ear about the many ways I could beat the government, get out of jail, and have my conviction overturned. This is part of the prison experience—guys with some experience in law hone in on your case and get you worked up about proving your innocence. John had worked in a law firm as a clerk. He was not a lawyer, but he knew how to read a law book and he knew how to bullshit. I actually rather enjoyed listening to him babble on about my case.

John weighed in at around three or four hundred pounds, give or take fifty, and he was a midnight eater, meaning he would wait until everyone had gone to bed before going to the microwave oven and cooking his shopping bag full of burritos that he would eat while watching television. John was a devout Christian and had covered his cube in religious icons that our camp counselor eventually deemed excessive and made him remove. John was suing the government for his religious freedoms over that one.

Anyway, John was pissing off my dog Steve big time. Steve had watched him in action when they were both over at the main camp and didn't appreciate the false hope he was spreading among the inmates. John would walk the yard, bending some poor guy's ear on how the government was screwing him and how John would file writs on his behalf and would arrange a pardon for this poor unsuspecting fish.

I have to say, in retrospect, that John would have made a killer lawyer had he gone that route instead of the path he took because he was convincing and a lot of what he said made perfect sense. Plus, his talk was very entertaining. Still, it was wrong to raise someone's hopes, especially when they were serving a long sentence.

Now, I knew John couldn't help himself talking law to anyone who would listen because John was compulsive at whatever he did. He would get on the stair-climber that was in front of the recreation office and walk for hours on that thing, taking little bitty steps. What amazed me was the stair-climber was located ten steps from the track where he could walk the same number of miles and actually go somewhere. But that was John's thing—I had my tango and John had his stair-climber. To each his own.

Still, John's legal bullshit bugged Steve and some of the other cons, so we came up with a plan to scare him straight. I had been visiting with Howard, the Cheyenne Indian who ran the sweat lodge with David. Howard's new job was the tool man at the garden shop where I would check out garden equipment and tools. He told me a story of how the inmates had once forged an indictment paper and served another inmate, charging him with a number of crimes and ordering him to appear in court. I asked Howard if he could do the same thing to John, and when he said he didn't see why not, the plan was set in motion.

It took a couple of weeks, but Howard obtained a copy of an indictment order, whited out the name, replaced it with John's, and listed the new charges. April 1 was fast approaching and the plan was moving forward. Howard had the documents ready to go and all that was left was to figure out the form of delivery. How were we going to serve John and make it look real? The most authentic way would have been to have control call John up to the main gate where he would be taken into an office and served formally by a CO. But that was out of the question because the papers were too real looking, and any officer would have to report it as a violation.

We thought it over between counts, and then Steve came up with the perfect solution. We would wait until mail call, and then Steve would drop it in John's cube like it came in the mail when he was away from his bed. As luck would have it, John left his cube before mail call and Steve had his chance.

"I did it," Steve reported, as he entered our cube. "I put it on his bed."

"Did he read it yet?" I asked.

"I'll go check," Steve replied as he left the cube.

I began looking over my stack of mail when Steve returned laughing silently to himself.

"What's happening?" I asked.

Steve was bursting as he whispered, "He is sitting on the bed staring at the thing. Man, he looks like he is about to cry."

"Let's go see him," I said, putting my mail on the desk. We walked into John's cube and there he was, just sitting and staring at the indictment. The look on John's ashen face told me the April Fools' joke was working better than we could have imagined. As the color drained from his face, the dead look in his eyes invoked a flood of sympathy from within my being. I knew that look all too well—it was the same expression I wore when I knew I was going to jail.

"What's up, John?" Steve asked as we sat down on his bed.

"I can't believe this. Look at what they are doing to me now," John replied, handing Steve the indictment.

Steve pretended to read it as John went on talking. "They can't do this to me. They are charging me with helping people with their legal work? I am protected by the Constitution. Since when is it illegal to help people?"

"Jeez, John, what are you going to do now? You were supposed to be going to the halfway house next month, weren't you?" I asked, trying hard not to laugh.

"Two weeks! I am supposed to be released in two weeks," John replied.

I thought that he was about to break down, and I guess Steve felt the same vibe, because he then told John what he really needed to hear.

"John, you know what I think about this?"

"What, Steve?" John appeared hopeful for the first

time, and grateful that Steve was actually talking to him as a friend.

Steve proceeded to tear the document up into little pieces. "This is bullshit. And it's also April Fools'!" John looked at us for a beat. Then it hit him. "You dirty bastards! You know, it just didn't look right. I couldn't believe they could charge me with doing legal work. You guys!" John suddenly became emotional, grabbed Steve, and gave him a big hug.

I stood and watched as Steve struggled to get free from the big Greek's grasp. John was overjoyed that the indictment was fabricated and he wasn't going to be bundled up and shipped off to some courtroom to face more jail time for trumped-up charges. John's happiness stayed with him right up until he left for the halfway house. He tried a few times to get back at us with the help of a female CO friend, but his attempts were feeble and we saw through all of them as we played along and had a good laugh each time.

John did quit helping people after that though. He wore out the stair-climber during his two final weeks in camp, and after he left, I swear I heard the thing breathe a sigh of relief. John called me about a month ago, telling me that he was in an office helping a lawyer friend with his practice. We promised to stay in touch and I am quite sure we will.

CHAPTER EIGHTEEN

Shih ho / Biting Through
Li / Chên

Getting to the truth of the matter.

I never broke any of the rules while I was incarcerated because I was a short-timer and all I had to do was keep my nose clean and not smoke any dope. I was offered drugs from the day I arrived until my time was up. I am sure that most of the people offering worked for the Feds, because right after the offers came in I would be summoned into the office for a pee test. They didn't test me at all for a good three months, but then I was tested almost every week.

The dangerous thing about being a prisoner in America is you don't have any rights. Some will argue that point with the prison personnel themselves and, even though they might have a valid argument, they almost always end up in the hole.

Prisoners are kept there for days, months, and years for breaking prison rules, which covers just about every conceivable infraction thought up by a group of sadistic, evil prison staffers. The rules varied from situation to situation, depending on who you were and why you were there.

And why *was* I arrested and put in jail? Was it really for selling bongs over the Internet? Or was it because I spoke out against the war in Iraq? I certainly had nothing to do with sales or shipping at the bong company, so how could I be guilty of the charge they accused me of, which was shipping bongs across state lines? Then why did I go to jail? According to the prosecution, I made movies that made fun of law enforcement, therefore I was a threat to society and should be locked up. This blatant use of power showed the Republicans at their worst.

Our Constitution guarantees freedom of expression and freedom of thought and freedom of religion. Isn't this why, according to the Republican Party, we are fighting in Iraq and elsewhere? We are supposed to be defending democracy and freedom, are we not? Isn't "freedom on the march," according to President Bush? I guess it's marching right out of America.

Resist not evil! This was the message I received when I was locked up. I kept hearing it over and over again. *Resist not evil!* Then it dawned on me: You don't have to fight anyone. All you have to do is just forgive your enemies for they obviously "know not what they do." When you think of it, if you forgive everyone, then you cannot have enemies. And without enemies, you no longer have reason to fight.

So the way to solve any problem is to understand what the problem is. And don't fight back. If someone steals your shirt then give him your coat as well. *Resist not evil.* It is a lesson that has taken me more than fifty years to learn, so I don't expect you readers to understand this or really any of my musings. That's the other lesson I learned while in jail: Expect nothing and you will never be disappointed.

Remember Nancy Reagan's catch phrase of the eighties, "Just say no"? Well, my slogan is "Just try it!" Try resisting the temptation to fight or argue with anyone. Try resisting the impulse to feel sorry for yourself. Instead, ask yourself, is this really worth fighting over?

The truth is, if you stay creative, you can overcome anything, because when you are creating you are working hand in hand with the muse, who judges not. The greatest hurdle one must overcome in this life is self-judgment, the critical eye, the demons that fill your head with doubts and fears. These are the shadows that disappear the minute you expose them to the light of understanding.

I was given a free pass into all the different societies that I encountered while I was in prison. I celebrated Jewish holidays, Christian holidays, and Muslim holidays. I sweated with the Indians, and eventually became a card-carrying Native American and found a way of life that I will follow now into the next world. I celebrated the Chinese New Year with the Chinese and broke bread with the Others, who were a group of South Pacific Islanders. I ate tacos and burritos with the homeboys from the barrios and delicious soul food with the brothers from South Central. I was treated with a respect I had never known before, and I learned how to exist in prison, a skill that would prove invaluable.

When your freedom is actually taken away from you simply because of who you are and not because of any criminal activity, something inside you changes. I imagine it must be similar to what a rape victim must feel in the sense that you have been violated, and it's a violation that you never forget. Since my arrest and imprisonment my life has changed considerably. I appreciate life so much more. But I watch what I say because I know how much effect words can have on the universe.

I almost messed up by accepting an invitation to perform in the annual Christmas show during my incarceration. When the gay barber who was in charge of the entertainment asked if I would do something in the show, I accepted immediately because I missed being onstage and was more than ready to kick some comedy ass. He asked me while I was standing in line at the commissary. I really didn't need to buy anything, but you get into a routine in prison, and standing in line was definitely part of the prison routine.

I started tripping on what I would do at the show. What bits could I do to entertain all these convicts? It is not as easy as you might think to perform in prison. For one thing, the inmates get all the television they can watch and they see all the comedians they need to see, so it isn't like they are entertainment deprived; if anything, they are overloaded with television.

But when it finally dawned on me that I was doing time and did not enjoy any freedom of speech, I quickly withdrew from the show. Man, that was a difficult decision for me, but the thought of the warden sitting in the audience, waiting for me to say something off-color or inappropriate, sent chills through my spine. And you know I would fuck up. I can't help myself. I was about to put myself in harm's way for a fucking Christmas show. I had no choice but to back out.

You don't appreciate the freedom that America supposedly guarantees until you lose it. The simple fact is, right now, we are all in the same boat. We all face the same enemy, which is ourselves. Not unlike Nazi Germany during the thirties, many Americans are standing by while the government is slowly dismantling the Constitution. The ironic thing about all of this is that American soldiers are dying in Iraq in the name of the very freedoms that are being suppressed here in America.

Our overcrowded jails are the direct result of the Republicans' war on anyone who disagrees with their policies. Have you noticed how little Americans protest the war? I should say wars. We are engaged in two expensive wars right now.

I saw a great interview with Gerald Ford, the U.S. president who pardoned Nixon. Donald Rumsfeld was his chief of staff when he was president, so the filmmakers wanted to hear Ford's take on how well Rummie was doing. Instead of the compliments one might expect, Ford lambasted Rumsfeld and the Bush administration for opening two fronts of war. "You finish one war before you start another," was his statement.

He was so right on! The filmmaker tried to get Ford off the subject, but old Gerald, whom I have nothing but respect for now, kept talking about how "everyone from Napoleon to Hitler knows what happens when you spread your troops thin like that." Everyone except Rummie, I guess.

When I was first released from prison, Steve wrote me for a while. Then I did not hear from him for about three months, when he finally called.

"Hey, dog, it's Steve," he said in his country singer's voice.

"Where you been, man?" I replied.

"Aw man, I just got out," Steve replied. "I just finished three more months. Remember how I told you the reason I did a year was because I did not want to be on 'paper' when I got out? Well, I was at home when my parole officer came by and told me I was not allowed to live where I was living."

"Where were you living?" I asked.

"With a buddy of mine," Steve answered sounding annoyed, as if I was the interrogator. "But the parole officer didn't like that I was back in the same place I was when I got busted."

"Were you?" I asked, annoying Steve further.

"Well, yeah. But I wasn't doing anything wrong. Anyway, he told me to move, so I moved, and then he called the cops on me for moving without permission."

"Wait, I don't understand—he told you to move and when you moved he violated you?"

"Well, I was supposed to let him see where I was moving before I actually moved. But I was so anxious to do what he advised that I just went ahead and moved. When I appeared before the judge, I told him I wasn't supposed to be on probation in the first place. He agreed because he was the one who sentenced me. He figured the prison had screwed up, but he told me he had no choice but to send me back for the violation. He was going to sentence me to one month and a year probation, but I asked how much would I have to serve to be free of probation. When he said three months I said I'd take it. And now it's all over and I am free! No more probation."

Steve went on to tell me how his ex-wife had wanted to sell their house while he was in prison, but I couldn't get past what I had just heard! He had done a year in jail just so he would not have to report to a probation officer when he was released, but because the prison made a typing error and filled in the wrong space with the wrong data, Steve had to go back to jail for another three months!

This American justice system is a joke—a stupid, evil joke—and believe me, someone will pay. And I don't mean in a violent way. I mean karma will right the wrongs.

The I Ching says the only thing constant in the universe is change, so no matter how fucked up the world looks now, we just have to wait and things will change. But remember, things will also change back, so don't get too comfortable.

There is an old Broadway song that says, "Do nothing till you hear from me." *That* is the message. Do nothing until you hear from God. This will give the universe time to heal the wounds and destruction caused by America's war on the world. Procrastination.

"Judge not lest ye be judged"; "Vengeance is Mine, sayeth the Lord"—the Bible has the answers to all of our questions if—and that is one big "if"—you know how to read the Bible. It seems like every organized religion agrees on only one thing: There is only one God even if it takes myriad forms. The problem is every religion feels it is their God who is favoring their dumb asses. The truth is, yes, there is only one God and only one human race. We, and I mean all of us, are God's chosen people, and we all are going to die, so why are we fighting and killing? I'll tell you why: because we have yet to evolve to the state of intelligent peace.

We have been uncovering traces of very intelligent, evolved people who knew what it was like to live in peace for centuries at a time. However, it is as if Earth is a school to learn how to share with others, and until we, as a people, learn that lesson, we are doomed to repeat the same stupid mistakes over and over.

When they arrested me, or rather when they raided my house and told me "I was not under arrest," I was told that if I took the government deal and pleaded guilty to whatever I was being charged with, I could go on with my life, which was entertaining people in night-clubs with my pro-pot act. However, if I defied the government and fought the charge in court with an attorney, they would not only imprison me, but they would also guarantee jail time for my wife and son. They promised me that if I didn't go quietly I would be in jail for at least two years and maybe longer. All of this for shipping a load of bongs across the state line to an undercover agent. There were no drugs involved, no illegal activity in my past history, and no record of any antigovernment protests. Nothing!

So much for free speech! The testimony of the prosecution showed me what a weak case they had against me. The Spirit kept whispering in my brain, "enjoy the experience" and "everything happens for a reason."

And now that I have survived nine months in prison and have finished writing this book, this part of my life is over. I am officially off probation. That means I can go about my business and I could smoke my weed without fear of incarceration if I wanted to. It also means I have my passport back so I can travel without having to obtain permission from the federal government.

We take these freedoms for granted, as well we should, because this is America, the land of the free. However, we are being ruled by a group of religious fanatics who disrespect our Constitution. Our Bill of Rights, which brave men and women are presently dying for as I write this, is being ignored. The sacred civil rights of American citizens are being violated every day by this bunch in power, and the only thing we can do is trust the universe. All wrongs will be corrected. It just takes time.

I want to thank everyone for reading my book. And I invite those who just flipped to this page to go back and read it. I had some great insights during my stay at Taft Correctional Institute. I am proud to have served my country and I am going to begin the fight to clear my name and to legalize my favorite herb.

This government has kindly opened the door for me, and I shall gladly take the opportunity to challenge its substance laws. These laws have filled America's prisons with millions of innocent victims. Now it is my turn to make a difference. I will do this with the direction of that higher power that has directed me all my life.

Via con Dios, my friends.

Acknowledge Him in all your ways.

ACKNOWLEDGMENTS

And with that, I thank my gorgeous, beautiful comedy partner and wife, Shelby, for being my sole inspiration and love for so much of my life; my children for being so beautiful, intelligent, and supportive during my ordeal, including my grandchildren, Morgan and Jack; my oldest daughter, Rae Dawn, for becoming the beautiful, talented actress who has appeared in more movies than her dad; my second-oldest daughter, Robbi, for becoming a top fashion model and an actress on the scary television series *Poltergeist*; my third and youngest daughter, Precious, for becoming a beautiful mother and a top solo performance artist; my cohort and pipe-making son, Paris, for going back to school and pursuing a university degree; and my younger son, Gilbran, for following in his father's footsteps and becoming a musician and a yoga teacher. A special thanks goes out to Maxine, my first wife and friend, who always had faith in me and supported my early career by holding down a job and paying the bills while I struggled to "make it;" to Toby Keene, husband of Robbi, whose art and talent and sense of humor always inspired me during my darkest days; and to Wes Berger, my other son-in-law, who married my daughter Precious and who produced my joy and new partner on the bongos, my grandson Jack.

I also want to thank my attorneys Richard Hirsch and Mike Nasatir, who did what they could with what they had, and Stanton Levenson, my Pittsburgh connection, who understood the injustice of it all and tried to do something about it. To Steve Gabrino for being a big supporter while I was in the joint. To Myra and her husband, Jillo, who gave their love and support to us during our ordeal; to Evelyn and Pat Morita for the phone call on the eve of my incarceration—I really needed that; to Ed Ruscha, America's greatest artist, who never forgot a friend and whose book kept reminding me who my friends were while I was locked up; to Michael and Brenda Satler, who mailed me all the latest Hollywood gossip rags; to John Lasker, who drove the many miles out to visit me during my "stay." A special thanks to Sharon Gavin and her daughter, Olivia, who wrote me and sent me beautiful drawings while I was gone; to my friend Rochelle and her daughter, Jade, who kept sending their love; to Jim and Valery Kalmason and their children, Jake and Leah, who kept me in their thoughts and prayers; and to Mark and Dianne Hanks and their beautiful children, Anna and Leland.

Thanks to my friend and agent Matt Blake at the Gersh Agency and Sara, his right-hand woman, and to Bob Gersh, who found work for me in spite of the odds.

And I have to thank Cheech Marin, my old partner—and I do mean old—for bringing Larry David out to the joint for a visit, and Bob Shay and Toby Emmric over at New Line for almost doing a movie with us. Thanks to David Goldman, who convinced *The Marijuana-Logues* to hire this old felon; and to Doug and Tony from the *'Logues*, who invited me into their world, giving me the center seat with love and honor; and to Ace, the producer of *The Marijuana-Logues*, for waiting patiently while I finished my probation before booking a United States tour. And a very special thanks to Lou Adler and his wife and boys for giving Cheech and me our start in the "business."

Thanks to Amy and her mom and dad, who sent me Will Henry's Western novels to read while I was "down," and to Stan Coleman for trying to make something of Cheech and Chong. Thanks to Forrest and her kids, who wrote me and encouraged me with their love and loyalty; to my sister, Nellie, and my brother, Stan, for not complaining when I wrote about our early life; and to Dr. John Joseph and his wife, Karen, for being great friends and consultants.

I want to especially thank Tom Warner and Marcie Carsey and the folks at *That '70s Show* for keeping my role as Leo open all during my incarceration. *That '70s Show* was the only job open to me when I got released from jail and I thank all the writers and producers and the cast for standing by me in my time of need. And I also want to thank Josh Gilbert, my friend who shot, produced, and edited *a/k/a Tommy Chong*, an award-winning documentary of this whole ordeal.

And now I want to thank Trish, my editor, who will probably be the only one reading this part of the book. Thank you, Trish, for making me look and read like a real writer. What a difference from my first rough draft, eh? And thank you, Bernie, my book agent, and Ian from New York, who has been waiting for, what, five years for this to happen? And I want to thank anyone whose name I did not mention because I forgot.

Thanks, Jay Leno, for your support while I was in jail and for having me on your show twice to tell my side. Big hug and thanks to Howard Stern and Robin for being in my corner and supporting me when everyone else deserted me. A huge thanks to Bill Maher for constantly reminding everyone how ridiculous this whole bust was. And thanks to Geraldo for sticking it to Mary Beth Buchanan about my jail sentence. Thanks also to Jon Stewart just in case he said something nice about me. And to Dave Chappelle for having me in his movie, in which I played a convict in jail.

Oh, and all the guys in Taft, whom I shall never forget, including Griff, my friend and drug counselor, and Ms. Strickland and the rest of the staff. And another thanks to Blind Steve, Jimmy the Harp Player, Jordan Belford, Smitty the Biker, Smitty the Fence Saver, David the Sweat Leader, David the Compost Maker, Jerry,

Harvey, all the Chicano brothers, all the Korean brothers, my Chinese brothers, and the Others. And to everyone who is presently incarcerated in America . . . my Peace I give unto you.

If I didn't mention your name, I do have an excuse. . . . I used to smoke way too much dope! Now I just enjoy life the way it is . . . straight. . . . Well, as they say, moderation in all things including moderation.